THE SERPENT'S STRATEGY

Hidden Systems of the World

A Spiritual Psychology of Deception and False Teachings

By: Natesha Monique Williams

Published By:

Living Life GOD's Way Publications LLC ™

THE SERPENT'S STRATEGY

Hidden Systems of the World

Spiritual Psychology, Deception, The Battle for the Mind

ISBN: 979-8-9941870-2-9

This book is published by:
Living Life GOD's Way Publications LLC ™

All Scripture quotations are taken from the **King James Version (KJV)** of the Bible.

The views and interpretations expressed in this work are those of the author and are intended for educational, spiritual, and informational purposes. This book is not intended to replace personal study, prayer, or wise counseling.

Published in the United States of America

Acknowledgment

This work is first and foremost an acknowledgment of the One from whom all truth proceeds God alone. Every revelation contained within these pages originates not from personal insight, but from the illumination of the Holy Spirit, who reveals what cannot be discovered through intellect alone. What has been written is the result of a divine uncovering—truth made visible where it was once hidden.

I acknowledge the Lord for His patience in this process, for the correction that refined my understanding, and for the clarity that replaced my ignorance. What began as questions became revelation, and what was once unclear has been brought into order through His guidance and wisdom.

I also acknowledge the role of endurance in this journey. Revelation is not given without a process, and understanding is not formed without refinement. There were moments of stretching, moments of self-confrontation, and moments where truth required the laying down of previously held perspectives. Each of those moments has shaped what is now written, the Lord continues to show he is GOD.

To my Husband, your presence and prayers have been both a covering and support. I thank God for your consistency and strength, through this call on my life you have been a steady foundation throughout this process. I love you to Life.

To my children and grandchildren, you are a reminder of purpose beyond words, and your lives carry the weight of what must be preserved and passed forward. I love you all to Life.

Finally, this acknowledgment extends to every reader. The willingness to engage, to reflect, and to examine what is written is not taken for granted. I am honored and humbled. This work was not written to be observed from a distance, but to be considered, processed, and, where necessary, allowed to confront the strategies the serpent may have used you to walk in ignorance. The Lord gives us all a chance to repent and get it right.

Truth does not require agreement to exist—but it does require openness to be received.

May the LORD bless you and keep you.

May He make his face shine upon you and be gracious to you

May He lift up His countenance upon you and give you peace

In Jesus, name……

Preface

Seeing What Was Always There

There are truths that do not reveal themselves through casual reading or surface-level observation. They require discernment, stillness, and a willingness to confront what lies beneath what appears familiar. This work was not written to introduce something new, but to uncover what has been present all along—patterns that have operated quietly within individuals, systems, and even within the structure of belief itself.

Throughout Scripture, the conflict between truth and deception is rarely presented as obvious opposition. More often, it appears as a combination of things, quiet distractions that reshape one's perception without immediately challenging their devotion. What may begin as influence eventually becomes an agreement, and what is agreed upon begins to define your identity. In this way, deception does not always remove truth, it repositions it.

This book examines those patterns.

It explores how spiritual language can coexist with psychological distortion, how systems can shape belief without being recognized, and how the human soul can be influenced in ways that feel natural while leading you away from alignment to God. It addresses the internal conflicts that arise when what is known does not match what is lived, and how those conflicts, if left unresolved, become the entry point for deeper deception.

At the center of this work is the understanding that transformation does not begin with behavior, it begins with your perception. What a person believes about God, about themselves, and about the systems around them will ultimately determine how they live, how they respond, and what they pursue. For this reason, the renewal of the mind is not optional; it is foundational.

These revelations were formed through a process of uncovering layer by layer the ways in which truth had been hidden by assumption, emotion, and inherited understanding. What is presented here is not an argument against faith, but a call to refine it. Not a rejection of devotion, but a realignment of it.

The goal is clarity.

Clarity concerning the nature of God.
Clarity concerning the condition of the soul.
Clarity concerning the systems that influence both.

This book will challenge your familiar ways of thinking. It will confront ideas that have been accepted without examination and expose patterns that often go unnoticed. At times, it may feel unsettling, not because it removes truth, but because it removes what has been layered around it.

Yet this is the purpose of revelation—to restore what has been altered and to return what has been displaced

As you read, I don't ask you to agree immediately, but to observe carefully. To consider not only what is written, but what it reveals within. Because the greatest transformations do not occur when information is added, but when perception is corrected.

What follows is not simply a study of Scripture or systems. It is an invitation—to see clearly, to discern accurately, and to return fully to the LORD.

Table Of Contents

The Architecture of Deception

Once the reality of the conflict is established, the next question is not whether deception exists, but how it operates. The war for the mind is not sustained through random thoughts or isolated moments of confusion. It is structured. It is reinforced. It is built.

Scripture reveals that deception does not merely appear—it is constructed.

In the book of Ezekiel, the Lord exposes a pattern that moves beyond individual error and into the formation of collective falsehood. What is uncovered is not simply the presence of false words, but the development of an entire system that people can live within while believing they are secure.

"They have seduced my people, saying, Peace; and there was no peace…"
— Ezekiel 13:10 KJV

The deception was not in open rebellion, but in reassurance. The people were not being led into obvious destruction, they were being stabilized in a false sense of safety. What was spoken sounded right. It felt right. It aligned with what they wanted to believe. Yet it was disconnected from truth.

The Lord describes this condition with precision. One builds a wall, and others cover it with untempered mortar. The structure appears complete. It looks finished. It gives the impression of stability. But its strength is an illusion.

This is the nature of deceptive systems.

They are not immediately recognizable as false because they are not empty. They are constructed using fragments of truth, reinforced by agreement, and presented with confidence. Over time, what was built becomes accepted, and what is accepted becomes normal.

People begin to live inside what was never established by God.

The danger is not only that the structure exists, but that it is trusted. Once trust is placed in what cannot stand, correction becomes difficult. The system no longer appears external it becomes the environment through which everything is interpreted.

This is where deception matures.

By the time Jesus addresses the Pharisees, the pattern revealed in Ezekiel has fully developed. What was once being built is now established, defended, and internalized.

"Ye are they which justify yourselves before men; but God knoweth your hearts…"
— Luke 16:15 KJV

The issue is no longer construction, it is justification.

The Pharisees were not outside the system; they were its representatives. They operated within a structure that appeared righteous, upheld religious order, and maintained external discipline. Yet beneath that structure was a misalignment between appearance and truth.

What had been built had now been accepted.
What had been accepted was now being defended.

Jesus exposes the core of the problem—not behavior alone, but perception. What is highly esteemed among men is an abomination in the sight of God. This statement reveals the final stage of deception. The system does not merely exist—it redefines value.

What is approved by people becomes the standard.
What is normalized becomes unquestioned.
What is questioned becomes rejected.

At this stage, truth is no longer the measure—agreement is.

This is how deception sustains itself.

It no longer needs to persuade. It only needs to maintain. Those within the system reinforce it, defend it, and perpetuate it, often without recognizing that what they uphold is misaligned with God.

The progression is consistent.

What begins as distortion becomes structure.
What becomes structure becomes environment.
What becomes environment becomes identity.

And once identity is formed within a system, separation from it feels like loss rather than freedom.

This is why deception is rarely confronted at the level of information. It must be confronted at the level of perception. A person must see differently before they can live differently.

Both Ezekiel and Luke reveal that the greatest danger is not open rejection of God, but confident misalignment with Him. It is possible to speak of peace where there is no peace, to uphold righteousness while redefining it, and to believe one is aligned with truth while operating within a system that has replaced it.

This is the Architecture of Deception.

It does not begin by removing truth—it begins by reshaping it.
It does not demand rejection—it invites adjustment.
It does not appear as darkness—it presents itself as light.

And because of this, it is not easily recognized.

Yet Scripture does not reveal these patterns to produce fear. It reveals them to produce discernment. To see not only what is being said, but what is being built. To understand not only what is believed, but what is forming the belief.

Understand that once the structure is recognized, it can no longer operate unnoticed.

And once it is no longer unnoticed, it can no longer remain unchallenged.

"Prove all things; hold fast that which is good."
— 1 Thessalonians 5:21 KJV

Not everything that appears right is from God.
Not everything that is accepted is truth.

"Believe not every spirit, but try the spirits whether they are of God..."
— 1 John 4:1 KJV

— Discernment is not optional, it is commanded…

This is why discernment is necessary.

You must Choose who you will serve……

Not everything that appears natural is without influence.
Not everything that feels harmless is without effect. And not every battle is visible.

"My people are destroyed for lack of knowledge: because thou hast rejected knowledge, I will also reject thee, that thou shalt be no priest to me..."
*— **Hosea 4:6 KJV***

INTRODUCTION

THE SERPENT'S STRATEGY: THE WAR FOR THE MIND

Before systems of government were formed, before cultures developed, and before human history unfolded as it is known today,

a conflict already existed.

It was not a conflict of nations, but of influence.
Not of weapons, but of thought.

Two systems emerged—unseen, yet governing the direction of humanity.

One is rooted in God—truth, order, and divine intelligence.
The other is rooted in rebellion—deception, distortion, and the elevation of self apart from God.

Both seek the same territory:

The mind.

Scripture reveals that this conflict is not natural, but spiritual.

"For we wrestle not against flesh and blood, but against principalities, against powers, against the rulers of the darkness

of this world, against spiritual wickedness in high places."
— Ephesians 6:12 KJV

From the beginning, this war has been fought through perception, belief, and internal dialogue. The serpent's first recorded strategy in the Garden of Eden was not force—it was influence.

"Yea, hath God said…?"
— Genesis 3:1 KJV

With a single question, the foundation of truth was challenged. Doubt entered. Perception shifted. And once perception changes, behavior follows.

What began in the mind resulted in the fall of humanity.

This pattern has not changed.

Ideas shape beliefs.
Beliefs shape decisions.
Decisions shape individuals, and individuals shape systems.

Entire societies are built upon ways of thinking—frameworks that determine identity, morality, and purpose. These systems often appear rational, beneficial, and even progressive, yet they can operate silently in opposition to truth.

The system of the world promotes independence from God, elevates emotion above truth, and encourages self-definition as the highest authority. The Kingdom of God calls for selfless surrender, the discipline of thought, and transformation through the word of truth.

These systems do not merge.
They do not align.
They stand in opposition.

The serpent, who initiated the first deception, has never relied on power—he has relied on influence. His strategy has always been to re-shape how humanity thinks so that people move away from God while believing they are moving toward freedom. Always remember he is a master at deception fighting to take your soul.

This is the foundation of spiritual deception.

Scripture reveals that deception is not limited to individuals—it operates through systems. Culture, philosophy, religion, politics, and economic structures can all become carriers of ideas that shape the human mind. This is why God's voice calls for obedience.

From the idolatry of ancient civilizations to the empires described throughout the Bible, Scripture consistently exposes how human systems can reflect a deeper spiritual influence watch the trickery.

Understanding this is not meant to produce anxiety, a friend of fear. It is meant to produce discernment. We as believers must exercise this gift to know the difference between good and evil study is key.

"But strong meat belongeth to them that are of full age, even those who by reason of use have their senses exercised to discern both good and evil..."

—Hebrews 5:14 (KJV)

"Be not conformed to this world: but be ye transformed by the renewing of your mind…"
— Romans 12:2 (KJV)

This book is written from the conviction that truth is revealed through the Word of God. The insights presented are not rooted in human theory, but in revelation gained through study of Scripture, given by the Holy Spirit and love for God and Jesus allowing the Word to interpret itself and expose patterns most often overlooked. He will use the foolish things of the world to confine wisdom.

(1 Corinthians 1:27) Each section examines how deception operates—through psychology, systems, and human ambition using biblical patterns to uncover how these influences continue to shape the world today.

Yet Scripture does not leave humanity in deception, it exposes truth.

At the center of the biblical narrative stands Jesus Christ—the One who exposes falsehood, restores truth, and renews the human mind.

"And ye shall know the truth, and the truth shall make you free."
— John 8:32 (KJV)

The purpose of this book is not simply to expose deception from the kingdom of darkness, but to equip you as a believer to recognize the levels on how the mind is influenced, to discern how systems shape perception, and to walk in the transformation that comes through alignment with the truth of God's Word this is true freedom.

The war is not distant.
It is not abstract.

It unfolds in thoughts, decisions, and beliefs every day.

This is the serpent's strategy.

Two systems.
One war.
And the battlefield is the mind.

CHAPTER ONE

HOW THE SERPENT THINKS

THE SERPENT'S STRATEGY –

A PSYCHOLOGICAL BLUEPRINT

Before temptation ever touches the body, it speaks to the mind, your every action begins as a thought long before it becomes behavior. The mind is the place where decisions are formed, where wisdom is received, where agreements are made, and where direction is established. Thoughts are the blueprints of obedience, and whoever writes the blueprint ultimately influences the outcome, your behavior always follows what has first been accepted internally.

We must know origin of the information being transferred.

"For to be carnally minded is death; but to be spiritually minded is life and peace."

— Romans 8:6 KJV

The serpent's strategy is built upon this law of thought and agreement. His warfare does not begin with visible action, but with suggestion—an idea introduced quietly, reinforced through repetition, and eventually solidified through belief. Once belief is established, behavior follows naturally, often without resistance, since the mind has already accepted what the body will later perform. In this way, the mind becomes the manufacturing plant of bondage, a fertile ground for producing cycles that feel natural even when they are rooted in deception of the delusion of the strategy.

When a thought is repeated long enough, it becomes conviction, conviction forms character, and character sustains cycles that repeat themselves over time. What appears to be personality is often the result of repeated internal agreements that have gone unchallenged.

"Now the serpent was more subtil than any beast of the field which the LORD God had made." — ***Genesis 3:1 KJV***

The nature of the serpent is not impulsive but strategic, not reactive but calculated. He does not rush into influence; he studies before he speaks and observes before he acts. He watches what triggers fear, what flatters pride, what weakens discipline, and what distracts faith, each of these becomes an open entry point into the mind.

His first weapon is not deception—it is data.

"From going to and fro in the earth, and from walking up and down in it." — ***Job 1:7 KJV***

This movement reveals intentional observation, not random activity. It reflects surveillance, study, and the gathering of information. Hell operates with precise structure, much like an intelligence system, where every failure becomes data and every wound becomes an access point. Nothing is ignored, everything is observed, recorded, and revisited and store into the cortex of the mind.

This is the foundation of **psycho-demography**—the mapping of human behavior, emotional patterns, and decision-making tendencies for the purpose of influence and exploitation. The serpent studies not only individuals, but patterns across time, observing how people respond under pressure, how they react emotionally, and how their emotional tendencies respond in cycles.

The adversary cannot read the mind, but he can chart your behavior. He cannot control the will, but he can study your responses.

When your emotion repeats, action often follows.
When behavior repeats, the outcomes reinforce themselves.

This is why repetition builds familiarity, and familiarity lowers resistance, allowing influence to operate more effectively over time.

"Be sober, be vigilant; because your adversary the devil, as a roaring lion, walketh about, seeking whom he may devour."

— 1 Peter 5:8 KJV

He does not devour without direction. He seeks whom he may—those whose patterns, habits, and repeated responses have created openings that can be used.

Modern culture reflects and amplifies the serpent's strategy.

Today's algorithms study behavior, advertisements mirror insecurities, and entertainment train's reaction before reflection, conditioning individuals to move by impulse while calling it authenticity. What once operated spiritually is now reinforced through systems, environments, and structures that shape how people think and respond. The serpent's main objective markets how his industry can profit from advertising.

"The heart is deceitful above all things, and desperately wicked: who can know it?"

— Jeremiah 17:9 KJV

The deceitful heart becomes the serpent's most effective industrial environment, on the grounds that he does not need new temptations when old emotions still produce the same responses. He feeds the ego until reason weakens, then guides individuals by feeling rather than faith, reinforcing cycles that continue without self-examination.

A person who responds the same way repeatedly becomes easier to study and easier to influence, this is why consistent patterns create recognizable pathways. What feels like comfort can become time consuming, giving exposure to what is trying to consume your soul. What is consistently repeated becomes easier to approach, easier to manipulate, and easier to reinforce. This is why we as believers must prioritize and become hunger for the word of God letting that be your targeted marketing strategy bring true wealth to your soul.

PSYCHO-DEMOGRAPHY —THE SERPENT'S DATA SYSTEM

The serpent's strategy operates through structured observation, gathering specific categories of behavioral data that allow influence to be applied with precision. These categories form a framework through which patterns are understood and reinforced. This is hell's counterfeit to the Lord's discernment. Where the Holy Spirit searches the heart to heal, the serpent studies your habits to deceive He builds his own analytics. Let's look at the data that is collected.

Emotional Data — The Measurement of Reaction

This refers to identifying what triggers immediate emotional responses such as anger, fear, offense, insecurity, or desire. Emotional data reveals where discernment is most easily bypassed, strong emotion often produces quick agreement without reflection. These moments become entry points where influence can be introduced before truth is considered.

The spirit of lust operates in this space.

What offends you the quickest?

Temporal Data — The Timing of Weakness

This involves recognizing specific times, seasons, or conditions where discipline weakens and spiritual awareness is reduced. Whether through fatigue, stress, isolation, or transition, these moments create openings where resistance is lower and influence can be applied more effectively.

What season weakens your prayer life and study time?

Relational Data — The Influence of Association

This examines the relationships, voices, and environments that shape thinking and decision-making. It identifies who or what has influence over perception, revealing whether those influences reinforce truth or indirectly shifting direction away from what's hidden.

Who or what influences your obedience?

Behavioral Data — The Patterns of Action

This tracks repeated interactions and habits, especially when those actions override conviction. Behavioral data exposes cycles more like an informer, they gather information, like what a person continually returns to, which becomes the clearest indicator of how they will respond in future situations. This is where idolatry often is formed and unhealthy relationships are placed above the Lord.

Which desires override your conviction?

"For as he thinketh in his heart, so is he."

— Proverbs 23:7 KJV

The serpent gathers these fragments until patterns become clear indicators of feedback. His goal is not possession, but conditioned agreement, where behavior aligns with established patterns without the need for constant external temptation. Once a cycle is established, the shift in the environment and memory begin to reinforce automatically. Only a complete cleaning and reboot from the Holy Spirit can help bring a fresh renewal to the mind.

"Lest Satan should get an advantage of us: for we are not ignorant of his devices."

— 2 Corinthians 2:11 KJV

You must recognize every device is a design, and every pattern reflects your prior agreement. What the world calls conditioning, Scripture reveals as bondage when it operates outside of truth.

The Lord dismantles the serpent's strategy through mind renewal. Where darkness builds cycles through history, God introduces transformation through revelation, interrupting patterns by restructuring your thoughts at its cognitive foundation.

"And be renewed in the spirit of your mind."

— Ephesians 4:23 KJV

Renewal is not motivational thinking; it is spiritual reformation. This truth becomes the new foundation of thought, replacing reaction with discernment and pattern with purpose.

"Let this mind be in you, which was also in Christ Jesus."

— Philippians 2:5 KJV

The mind of Christ cannot be mapped through human patterns, given it is governed by obedience rather than emotion, and by purpose rather than pride. It does not follow cycles; it follows truth.

"And ye shall know the truth, and the truth shall make you free."

— John 8:32 KJV

You must understand that freedom is not the absence of struggle, it is the mastery of liberty. A renewed mind does not react automatically—it discerns, evaluates, and responds through truth.

"But he that is spiritual judgeth all things... But we have the mind of Christ."

— 1 Corinthians 2:15–16 KJV

When a believer begins to think differently, the serpent loses access to familiar pathways. Cycles weaken, patterns collapse, and what once produced the same outcome no longer functions in the same way. You begin to walk in the newness that God has promise.

THE SERPENT'S STRATEGY – THE CHOICE OF SYSTEMS

Every decision is worship, and every reaction is allegiance. The serpent builds through analysis, studying your behavior to establish his influence, while God builds through awareness, revealing truth that produces freedom to live a life of victory.

Two systems continue to contend for the same ground. The serpent offers control without peace, while God offers surrender that produces dominion walk in your authority. Whichever system shapes your thought will ultimately write the script to your destiny.

"Choose you this day whom ye will serve..."

— Joshua 24:15 KJV

The war begins in the mind, but victory begins in renewing the mind. Let this be the moment where awareness produces transformation, where patterns are destroyed, and where thinking is rebuilt in alignment with the Word of God.

The Serpent's Strategy Insight

The serpent has studied generations, but he cannot master a mind that walks in revelation of the word of God. He can observe behavior, but he cannot control a believer who refuses to respond from established patterns. Every renewed thought closes a door that was once open, and every shift in perception disrupts a strategy that once operated unnoticed. Where reaction once governed, discernment now leads. Where fear is once dictated and governed, truth now directs and rules. The mind that is surrendered to God no longer operates according to past cycles, but according to present revelation. This is where the serpent's strategy fails, not due to pressure disappearing, but so patterns no longer produce the same results. One small compromise can slow progression to live.

PRAYER

Father,
I thank You for exposing the invisible systems that have influenced my thoughts. Today I chose that my mind be renewed and crucify my flesh not to react to its strategies. Give me revelation over repetition, and truth over deception. Rebuild my inner world until every false pattern collapse and every thought aligns with Your Word.

I surrender my logic to Your wisdom and my emotions to Your peace. Strengthen my discernment so that I recognize what seeks to influence me and give me the discipline to reject what does not come from You. Let my mind be transformed, my perception be aligned, and my responses be governed by truth.

Let every pattern that has operated against Your will be destroyed at the root and establish within me a way of thinking that reflects the mind of Christ.

In Jesus name,

Amen.

PROPHETIC DECREE

I decree that the serpent's strategy no longer finds access in my thinking.
My responses are no longer shaped by past patterns.
My emotions are no longer used as instruments of influence.

My mind is renewed, anchored in truth, and governed by the Spirit of God. I do not respond according to reoccurrences I respond according to revelation.

Darkness cannot trace my thoughts.
Deception cannot shape my perception.
Fear cannot guide my decisions.

I walk in clarity, I walk in authority, and I walk in truth. The war for my mind is settled through renewal, and I live in the victory established through Christ.

In Jesus name, it is established.

CHAPTER TWO

EVE THE FIRST MIND TARGET

THE BATTLE WAS PSYCHOLOGICAL, NOT PHYSICAL

The Garden

In the garden, before sin ever expressed itself through conduct, a conversation had already reshaped perception, what eventually manifests outwardly is first negotiated inwardly. The serpent did not begin with rebellion, nor did he initiate his strategy through intensity or direct opposition, instead, he began with reasoning, carefully introducing a form of communication designed to shift the interpretation before it ever shaped the outcome.

Every deception that has existed since that moment follows this same architecture, words that appear harmless, questions that seem thoughtful, and ideas that invite evaluation rather than obedience. The first war was not fought in Heaven's throne room, nor was it first revealed through open conflict, but in the hidden corridors of the thoughts of the mind, where perception became the battlefield and agreement became the objective.

Eve's mind became the proving ground of two systems, revelation and reasoning, obedience and observation, God's truth and human interpretation. What unfolded in Eden was not merely a moment of disobedience, but the unveiling of a strategy that would be repeated across generations. This teaches a truth most people will not speak today.

"Now the serpent was more subtil than any beast of the field which the LORD God had made. And he said unto the woman, Yea, hath God said, Ye shall not eat of every tree of the garden?"

— Genesis 3:1 KJV

The first temptation did not begin with appetite or desire, but with analysis. The serpent introduced the idea that God's divine instruction could be evaluated rather than obeyed, shifting the role of the human mind from agreement to assessment. Eve's mindset, aligned with trust, was now invited to interpret what had already been established. This destabilizes the target's certainty.

The LORD had formed her consciousness through communion, where reality was understood through relationship with God rather than independent reasoning. Yet now another voice entered that internal dialogue, and that voice did not begin with contradiction, but with a question. That question did not immediately overthrow truth, but it created a distance from it, and the distance in thought gradually becomes distance in obedience. Her feelings were the prize.

"For God doth know that in the day ye eat thereof, then your eyes shall be opened, and ye shall be as gods, knowing good and evil." — ***Genesis 3:5 KJV***

Knowledge became the bait, but not knowledge rooted in submission to the word of God, knowledge separated from dependence on God. The serpent offered her the illusion that understanding apart from obedience was enlightenment, presenting independence as growth and self-governance as wisdom.

The war for Eden was fought in the unseen realm of thought—a collision between trust and curiosity, instruction and interpretation. Eve did not fall because she lacked strength, but because she attempted to step into wisdom without remaining connected to the presence that gives wisdom meaning.

The thought carried its own justification, presenting itself as insight rather than departure. Authority shifted without announcement; what was once received from God was now being weighed by the mind. In that exchange, truth was no longer the starting point but the subject of evaluation, and once instruction is treated as something to weigh, obedience begins to weaken.

WHEN GOD'S WORD BECOMES OPEN TO INTERPRETATION

"Add thou not unto his words, lest he reprove thee, and thou be found a liar."

— Proverbs 30:6 KJV

Every deception begins the moment God's Word shifts from final authority to optional interpretation. Eve's reasoning did not begin with denial; it began with revision, and revision is often more dangerous than rejection because it appears close to truth while quietly altering it.

"We may eat of the fruit of the trees of the garden: But of the fruit of the tree which is in the midst of the garden, God hath said, Ye shall not eat of it, neither shall ye touch it, lest ye die."

— Genesis 3:2–3 KJV

The phrase "neither shall ye touch it" was never spoken by God, yet the information entered her thought as if it were part of the original command. This small addition transformed instruction into interpretation, and once the Word became flexible in her mind, her conviction began to lose its stability. This same pattern continues among believers today, where obedience is often replaced with explanation, and clarity is toned down through interpretation. Instead of aligning fully with what God has spoken, the mind begins to negotiate with it, creating space between truth and application.

DESIRE REDIRECTED TOWARD DISOBEDIENCE

"And when the woman saw that the tree was good for food, and that it was pleasant to the eyes, and a tree to be desired to make one wise, she took of the fruit thereof, and did eat, and gave also unto her husband with her; and he did eat."

— Genesis 3:6 KJV

Desire itself was never the issue; we must understand God created appetite and longing as part of the human design. The serpent did not create desire, he redirected it, shifting its focus from communion with God to curiosity about self. This shift comes after disobedience is in play.

The same desire that once drew Eve toward the Creator was now redirected toward creation, and in doing so, the object of fulfillment changed. Psychologically, the serpent reframed satisfaction, presenting obedience as limitation and curiosity as liberation, making what was once forbidden appear very appealing rather than dangerous.

Temptation did not succeed by introducing something entirely new, but by assigning a new purpose to what already existed within her. This is one of the greatest strategies....

AGREEMENT PRECEDES ACTION

Before Eve reached for the fruit, she had already reached a conclusion within her mind. We must always watch what we desire, make sure it aligns with God's will for your life. Agreement is always the birthplace of a person's actions. This is because what the mind accepts, the body eventually follows.

"Can two walk together, except they be agreed?"

— Amos 3:3 KJV

Every fall begins with a mental agreement. The strategy does not force disobedience—it persuades it until agreement is formed. That persuasion unfolds through internal dialogue, where thoughts interact, respond, and eventually reshape what is considered true. The serpent's greatest victory was not Eve's action, but her internal agreement. Once deception becomes conviction, rebellion no longer feels like rebellion—it feels justified, even enlightened.

SELF-DECEPTION AND THE LOSS OF COVERING

"And the eyes of them both were opened, and they knew that they were naked; and they sewed fig leaves together, and made themselves aprons." — ***Genesis 3:7 KJV***

This is where awareness came, but it was not the spiritual enlightenment that had been promised. They gained information, but in doing so, they lost their innocence. The moment the mind absorbed knowledge outside of obedience, the soul lost its covering, and what followed was not empowerment, but an awaking to deception.

Now this is one of the more cunning strategies that believers need to always watch and pray for. **Self-deception** always presents itself as enlightenment, but it ultimately produces vulnerability. Eve believed she was ascending into wisdom, yet what she encountered was the weight of awareness without the protection of truth.

Their response was immediately, they attempted to cover themselves, sewing fig leaves together in an effort to manage what had been exposed. This became the first expression of religion, humanity attempting to solve spiritual conditions through self-designed solutions. Religion, in this context, is thought without transformation and effort without intimacy. When the mind attempts to manage what only grace can cleanse, it produces a system instead of surrender.

"There is a way which seemeth right unto a man, but the end thereof are the ways of death." — ***Proverbs 14:12 KJV***

Every system built on self-reliance traces its origin back to this moment. This is psychological influence wrapped in religion.

This is why Jesus taught against religion a system set up by man-made logic that will keep you in a cycle of unbelief which leads to disobedience. Don't trade God's command for opinions of man.

In **Mark Gospel 7:6–8**, Jesus confronts this directly:

"This people honoureth me with their lips, but their heart is far from me. Howbeit in vain do they worship me, teaching for doctrines the commandments of men."

Here the issue is not the absence of worship, but the source of it. Worship continued, language remained correct, and structure was intact—but the origin had shifted from God to man. This is the final stage of deception, when human instruction is received as God's divine truth.

In **Matthew Gospel 23:23**, He exposes the imbalance:

"...and have omitted the weightier matters of the law, judgment, mercy, and faith..."

They maintained high standards in minor practices while neglecting the nature of God Himself. This reveals a critical pattern; systems often preserve what is measurable while abandoning what is spiritual.

The serpent's advantage is in trying to merely make people disobey God, and in training them to believe they are obeying Him while remaining disconnected from Him.

In **John Gospel 5:39–40**, Jesus exposes the deepest layer:

"Search the scriptures... and they are they which testify of me. And ye will not come to me, that ye might have life."

The Scriptures were present, yet the source of it was rejected. Knowledge increased, but the relationship was refused. This is not ignorance—it is misalignment disguised as devotion.

This is the system –

- Truth becomes studied but not submitted to
- Worship becomes expressed but not lived
- Authority shifts from God to spiritual hypocrisy
- Identity forms around practice rather than transformation

What began with Eve as a question— *"Hath God said"?* Evolved into a system where men answered that question for themselves.

WHY GOD ALWAYS RETURNS TO THE MIND

"And the LORD God called unto Adam, and said unto him, Where art thou?"

— ***Genesis 3:9 KJV***

This question was never about a physical location; it was directed toward awareness and spiritual insight. God was not searching for their bodies; He was addressing their thinking.

"Where are you in your understanding? Where has your reasoning taken you?"

Before restoring relationship, God confronts reasoning, the reason is that behavior is only the outward expression of what has already been accepted inwardly. This is why Jesus began His ministry with the command:

"Repent, for the kingdom of heaven is at hand."

— ***Matthew 4:17 KJV***

Repentance is not merely sorrow, it is transformation of heart and thought you must turn away and leave the old way to start a new way, founded on the truth of God's word as the foundation. The Holy Spirit gives wisdom where spiritual vision is restored. Deliverance without mental renewal does not produce freedom, it only rearranges bondage keeping one unaware.

God still asks every generation the same question:
Where are you thinking from?

WHAT EDEN TEACHES HUMANITY

Humanity's first responsibility is not external expression, but it is internal development. Before one can accomplish anything outwardly, one must guard the structure of one's own perception.

Eve reveals that the serpent does not always approach with confrontation, but with conversation—familiar, engaging, and seemingly harmless. This is why vigilance must extend beyond actions to thoughts. *"Keep thy heart with all diligence, for out of it are the issues of life."*

— Proverbs 4:23 KJV

To guard the heart is to monitor the mind, thoughts are seeds, and when they are left unexamined, they develop into imagination that eventually produce actions.

Spiritual vigilance is the discipline of refusing to entertain what contradicts what God has already made clear. This is where humanity falls when curiosity replaces conviction, but they rise when discernment replaces debate.

HOW THIS PATTERN REAPPEARS IN LEADERSHIP, TEACHING, AND CULTURE

Every modern distortion of truth follows the same pattern established in Eden. Leadership fails when reasoning replaces revelation, teaching declines when interpretation overshadows inspiration, and culture weakens when desire is elevated above truth.

"Professing themselves to be wise, they became fools."

— Romans 1:22 KJV

The serpent's philosophy has not changed—it has only adapted its appearance. It now speaks through intellectual systems, cultural movements, and even spiritual platforms, yet the message remains the same, independence from God presented as wisdom.

Humanity continues to pursue knowledge without accountability, influence without intimacy, and surrender without submission.

The structure remains consistent: observation, manipulation, counterfeit, and vain repetition.

THE LASTING LESSON OF THE FIRST MIND TARGET

Eve was not simply deceived, she was studied. Her response became a model, a pattern that would be revisited and replicated across generations.

Yet her story does not end in defeat—it points toward redemption.

"And I will put enmity between thee and the woman, and between thy seed and her seed; it shall bruise thy head, and thou shalt bruise his heel."

— Genesis 3:15 KJV

The same pathway that was first targeted became the pathway through which redemption entered. The serpent struck the heel, but Christ crushed the head—the seat of reasoning, the place where deception begins.

Victory was established in the very arena where the battle first unfolded, the mind.

The Serpent's Strategy Insight

The serpent's strategy has always been rooted in observation and influence, not power. What is understood can be approached, and what is repeated can be reinforced. Through the study of patterns,

he builds frameworks of influence that rely on familiarity and internal agreement.

However, while he can study behavior, he cannot govern a mind that is anchored in revelation knowledge of the truth of the word. Every renewed thought disrupts a pattern that once operated freely, and every alignment with truth removes access that was previously available.

Where agreement once formed unconsciously, discernment now stands as a guard. The mind that is surrendered to God no longer functions according to past cycles, but according to present truth, and this is where the serpent's strategy begins to fail—when patterns are no longer followed, and responses are no longer shaped by previous agreements.

PRAYER

Father,
I thank You for revealing the patterns that began in Eden and for exposing how deception operates within the mind. Heal every place where reasoning has replaced revelation and restore within me a clarity that is rooted in Your truth.

Teach me to recognize the voice that questions what You have already spoken and give me the discipline to remain aligned with Your Word without compromise. Strengthen my discernment so that I do not entertain what seeks to distance me from truth and renew my thinking so that my perception remains anchored in You.

Let my mind be a place of communion, not confusion, and establish within me a way of thinking that reflects obedience, clarity, and trust.

In Jesus name,

Amen

PROPHETIC DECREE

I decree that my mind is anchored in truth and governed by revelation.
I do not interpret what God has made clear—I align with it.

The serpent's voice finds no agreement in my thoughts.
Every pattern of reasoning that opposes truth is destroyed.

I discern before I decide, and I obey without compromise.
My perception is restored, my thinking is renewed, and my mind is aligned with the mind of Christ.

I walk in clarity, I walk in authority, and I walk in truth.
The first battlefield is now my place of victory.

In Jesus name, it is Amen…

CHAPTER THREE

THE YOUNG PROPHET

The War Between Voice and Will

Obedience is not merely a moral decision or an outward act of discipline, it is a mental alignment that determines how the mind responds to truth when it is placed in tension with emotion, fatigue, or external influence. Every command of God becomes a test, not simply of behavior, but of interpretation revealing whether the mind will remain anchored in revelation or begin to negotiate through reasoning.

In ***1 Kings 13***, the account of the young prophet reveals far more than a moment of disobedience; it exposes the internal anatomy of deception, demonstrating how a divinely called mind can still be influenced when the voice of familiarity begins to outweigh the voice of God. The battle is not visible, but inward, unfolding in the space where thought, trust, and will intersect.

"For rebellion is as the sin of witchcraft, and stubbornness is as iniquity and idolatry."
— ***1 Samuel 15:23 KJV***

Disobedience never begins with action; it begins as a negotiation within the mind, where logic attempts to reposition revelation and reasoning begin to challenge what was once accepted without question. The serpent's original question in Eden— *"Hath God said?"*—continues to echo through every believer who begins to internally negotiate what God has already made clear. Within the life of the young prophet, we observe a consistent psychological pattern, divine command, external contradiction, internal conflict, and eventual collapse. The progression is not random, it is structured, and it reveals that the serpent's strategy does not always appear as open temptation; at times, it arrives as validation that feels spiritual, reasonable, and even justified.

DIVINE INSTRUCTION AS SPIRITUAL PSYCHOLOGY

THE CALL AND THE COMMAND

The story begins with clarity, as God gives the young prophet a precise and uncompromising instruction:

"Eat no bread, nor drink water, nor turn again by the same way that thou camest."
— 1 Kings 13:9 KJV

This command was not merely restrictive; it was deeply intentional, functioning as a form of spiritual and psychological training. God was shaping the prophet's mind to operate beyond dependence on comfort, routine, or environmental influence. Food represented sustenance and satisfaction, while direction represented control and familiarity, both of which are deeply rooted human instincts.

To deny both was to train the mind to rely entirely on divine instruction rather than natural impulse.

Every command from God carries psychological weight. Obedience is not only about alignment with instruction; it is about transformation of internal patterns. Through obedience, God detoxes the mind from the conditioning of the world, breaking cycles that have been formed through repetition and familiarity.

From a psycho-demographic perspective, obedience disrupts behavioral continuity. The serpent studies repetition, as a result of repeated behavior that creates patterns that can be approached and influenced. However, obedience that operates beyond comfort interrupts those patterns, making the believer more difficult to study and less accessible to influence. This was God's intention,to shape a prophet whose discernment would outweigh his desire, whose obedience would remain intact regardless of circumstance. The young prophet began in alignment, but obedience that has not been tested has not yet been proven.

THE COUNTERFEIT VOICE –

DECEPTION THROUGH FAMILIARITY

The narrative shifts when an older prophet, having heard of the young man's actions, seeks him out and finds him resting beneath an oak tree. This detail is not incidental—it reveals a moment of vulnerability. Fatigue does not simply weaken the body; it alters how the mind processes information, often increasing the desire for reassurance and validation.

The old prophet approaches with language that appears credible:

"*I am a prophet also as thou art; and an angel spake unto me by the word of the LORD.*"
— ***1 Kings 13:18 KJV***

Here, deception does not come in opposition—it comes through familiarity. The voice that contradicts God does not present itself as foreign, but as recognizable, aligned, and authoritative. In spiritual warfare, imitation rarely appears in contrast; it appears in resemblance. The young prophet's respect for shared identity overrode his adherence to divine instruction. This moment reveals a critical psychological dynamic, he was not deceived because he lacked knowledge of what God said, but because he desired confirmation that aligned with his current condition.

Fatigue does not seek truth, it seeks permission.

The old prophet's deception demonstrates how influence often operates through trusted structures. When identity becomes a source of validation, obedience becomes negotiable, and the clarity of God's voice is weighed against the familiarity of human affirmation. This is one of the serpent's most refined strategies, creating agreement around disobedience in a way that feels spiritually justified. When God speaks, He confirms it.

HOW PARTIAL OBEDIENCE OPENS THE DOOR

THE PSYCHOLOGY OF DELAY

When the young prophet chose to sit and eat, he did not simply break a command; he stepped out of alignment with divine rhythm. Obedience is not only about action, but also about timing. Every instruction from God carries a sequence, and when that sequence is interrupted, the structure that sustains it begins to shift.

"To obey is better than sacrifice, and to hearken than the fat of rams."
— 1 Samuel 15:22 KJV

The moment he engaged in partial obedience, the environment changed. The same voice that deceived him became the voice through which judgment was declared. This reveals a powerful principle, God does not contradict Himself, but He may use the same environment that exposed disobedience to reveal its consequences. Even in judgement, God still show mercy.

The lion that met the prophet on the road did not behave naturally, it did not devour the body, nor harm the donkey. This was not random, it was symbolic. The lion represented judgment that was precise, controlled, and instructional rather than disorderly.

From a psycho-demographic perspective, consequences are not merely punishment, they are information. They reveal patterns, expose misalignment, and provide data that can be used for transformation. What is not corrected becomes a pattern, and what becomes a pattern extends beyond the individual into future generations. The young prophet's failure became more than a moment, it became a case study in obedience, demonstrating that a mind that compromises halfway is already being reshaped by disobedience. Sometimes obedience means walking away from a table you are invited to sit and eat your obedience matters more.

CONSEQUENCES AND CORRECTION –

GOD'S DISCIPLINE AS DIVINE ALIGNMENT

The image of the lion and the donkey standing beside the prophet's body is one of the most profound symbolic moments in Scripture. It reflects a tension between power and restraint, judgment and mercy, demonstrating that God's correction is never without purpose.

"For whom the Lord loveth he chasteneth, and scourgeth every son whom he receiveth."
— Hebrews 12:6 KJV

Correction is not rejection, it is alignment. God did not erase the young prophet's calling; He preserved his story as instruction. His life became a psychological mirror through which every believer can examine their own obedience. Obedience is not proven when revelation is received, it is proven when self-discipline is required.

The serpent studies appetite, identifying where desire overrides discipline, while God measures attention, observing whether the mind remains fixed on truth when alternative voices arise. The young prophet's body fell silent, but his story continues to speak with clarity, sincerity is not a defense against deception; only submission is. Modern psycho-demographic analysis reflects the same reality—human behavior is most vulnerable when urgency and fatigue intersect, this is why these conditions reduce resistance and increase susceptibility to influence. When believers cease resting in truth, they begin negotiating with imitation. That is where the craftiness of satan begin.

CHRIST'S EXAMPLE — PERFECT OBEDIENCE RESTORES AUTHORITY

Where the young prophet faltered, Christ demonstrated perfection. The temptations in the wilderness reflect the same psychological structure—offers of provision, validation, and proof—yet each was met with unwavering obedience.

"Man shall not live by bread alone, but by every word that proceedeth out of the mouth of God."
— Matthew 4:4 KJV

Christ did not respond from need, emotion, or external validation; He responded from identity. His obedience was not reactive; it was rooted in faith and obedience to his master. He did not require confirmation from another voice, because His alignment with the Father was complete.

Through this, Christ dismantled the psychological pattern of deception, demonstrating that a mind anchored in truth cannot be moved by alternative voices.

He restored what was compromised, establishing a model of obedience that is not influenced by condition or circumstance.

This is the mind of Christ—a mind that does not negotiate with deception because it does not seek validation outside of truth.

The Serpent's Strategy Insight

What is revealed in this account is not merely a moment of deception, but a pattern of influence that continues across generations, where the mind is approached not through opposition, but through familiarity, timing, and internal vulnerability, exposing the reality that the greatest threats to alignment are rarely external attacks, but internal permissions formed under the appearance of agreement.

The young prophet was not overpowered; he was persuaded at a moment when fatigue weakened discernment and familiarity replaced authority, revealing that spiritual compromise does not begin with open rebellion, but with subtle shifts in what the mind allows to stand alongside what God has already established, because deception becomes effective not by sounding false, but by sounding close enough to truth that it is not immediately rejected.

The danger was not ignorance, but misplaced trust, because the voice that contradicted God did not appear as an enemy, but as someone who understood his calling, and this exposes a critical principle: influence gains access where trust is extended without verification, and what is not tested becomes a doorway for what is not aligned.

This is how influence bypasses resistance, not by confronting truth directly, but by repositioning it through something that feels recognizable, something that carries the tone of alignment without the substance of it, allowing what is foreign in origin to appear internal in acceptance, and once accepted internally, it no longer feels like influence—it feels like reasoning.

That transition is where the real shift occurs.

Because the moment something external is received as internal information, it is no longer resisted, it is processed, and once it is processed, it begins to shape the response, not as something imposed or forced, but as something concluded.

What has already been established does not require reconsideration, yet once it is revisited, it is no longer held with the same authority, because it has been moved from position to an alternative, and once truth becomes an option, it no longer governs it competes.

And truth was never designed to compete.

This is what made the situation with the young prophet in First Kings 13 so precise, because the instruction had already been given with clarity, yet the contradiction did not present itself as defiance, but as justified, revealing that deception does not remove truth surrounding it, reducing its exclusivity by introducing options that appear equally valid. Nothing was taken from him; something was added, and that addition altered the entire structure, since what stands alone carries authority, but what stands beside something else must now be weighed, and once weighing begins, obedience is no longer immediate it becomes conditional.

And conditional obedience is no longer obedience, it is negotiation.

This is where the spiritual breakdown occurs, not in the rejection of truth, but in the reclassification of it, seeing that what was once absolute is now subject to reasoning, and reasoning opens the door for preference, and preference weakens the alignment.

The failure was not that he did not know it was that he allowed what he knew to be processed again, and in doing so, he shifted from responding to truth to evaluating it, and once truth is evaluated, it can be adjusted to fit what has been newly accepted.

This is why obedience must remain continuous, considering that it is not sustained by the memory, but by present alignment, and what has been given must remain in position without being reopened, on account of every reopening reintroduces the possibility of alteration, and what can be altered can no longer preserve what it was meant to establish. A mind that remains anchored does not revisit what has already been settled, because stability is not maintained by repeated consideration, but by consistent alignment, and in that alignment, there is no space for contradiction to establish itself, considering it is not given the position required to operate.

This is where influence loses its strength, not because it ceases to speak, but because it is no longer received, and what is not received cannot take form, and what cannot take form cannot direct outcome.

Over time, this produces a structural shift within the mind, where what once required discernment becomes immediately recognized, and what once required resistance no longer reaches the level of engagement, not because it is weaker, but because it is no longer given access to operate at all.

And this is where the underlying operation becomes clear.

As a result of what was working beneath the surface was not merely suggestion, but manipulation structured through deceit, where manipulation positioned the influence to appear aligned, and deceit concealed its contradiction long enough for agreement to form, and once agreement was formed, the outcome was no longer determined by what was true, but by what had been accepted. This reveals that spiritual warfare is not centered on what is heard, but on what is allowed to remain, this is why what remains will eventually shape the response, and what shapes a response will determine the direction, and direction will always produce a consequence.

This is one level spiritual warfare. The battle within.

PRAYER

Father,

I surrender every tendency within me that seeks to reason with what You have already spoken. Teach me to obey even when comfort argues, and to remain aligned with Your voice when other voices appear familiar, credible, or persuasive. Silence every influence that attempts to reposition Your Word and deliver me from the need for confirmation that replaces trust. Renew my mind so that I value instruction more than affirmation and strengthen me in moments of fatigue where compromise begins to feel reasonable. Heal every place in me where I have negotiated with clarity and restore within me a steadfastness that completes what You have commanded. Make me consistent in obedience, alert in discernment, and faithful in every condition.

In Jesus name, Amen.

PROPHETIC DECREE

I decree that the voice of the serpent finds no agreement within me. My obedience remains firm, my discernment is clear, and my spirit is aligned with truth.

I do not yield to familiarity that contradicts God, nor do I seek validation outside of His Word. Let every counterfeit voice be exposed, and every influence that opposes truth removed.

My mind is renewed, my steps are ordered, and my obedience is complete.
I walk in the mind of Christ, governed by truth, sustained by peace, and established in submission.

The serpent's strategy is destroyed, and the voice of the LORD prevails in my life.

In Jesus Name

CHAPTER FOUR

IMITATION WITHOUT AUTHORITY: THE ILLUSION OF POWER

The Mechanics of Imitation

When Moses and Aaron walked into Pharaoh's court, they entered more than a throne room; they entered a living system of belief. Egypt was a nation built on rituals, symbols, and the mastery of perception. Power there did not rest on truth but on control—control of what the people saw, repeated, and expected. God sent His servants into that atmosphere for the reason that His authority never hides from imitation; it exposes it.

"Then Pharaoh also called the wise men and the sorcerers: now the magicians of Egypt, they also did in like manner with their enchantments."
— ***Exodus 7:11 KJV***

The scene was more than a contest of miracles. It was a confrontation between *authentic authority* and *a replicated technique.* Pharaoh's magicians did not deny what they saw; they duplicated it. They understood that resemblance weakens reverence. If a copy can appear convincing, the mind begins to question the original. This is the oldest strategy of the serpent, to manufacture similarity so that certainty dissolves.

Every person who witnessed the magician's imitation experienced the same psychological tension that still operates today when two things look alike, the brain conserves energy by choosing familiarity over examination.

The serpent manipulates this law of perception by flooding the world with options that appear spiritual but lack origin in God. In Pharaoh's court, the counterfeit served a political purpose; in modern life, it serves a psychological one. Both seek the same outcome, to delay discernment.

This is where you begin to question truth. The rod in Aaron's hand became a serpent by divine command, a transformation rooted in obedience. The rods in the magician's hands became serpents by manipulation, a replication rooted in rebellion. One act was born from a genuine relationship, the other from ritual founded in deceit. And yet, to the untrained eye, both appeared equal. That is how deception hides, not by opposing truth, but by standing close enough to it that at a distance it becomes hard to measure.

"And Pharaoh's heart was hardened, neither did he hearken unto them; as the LORD had said."
— ***Exodus 7:13 KJV***

Imitation hardens the heart in response to numb the need for obedience. When everything seems spiritual, conviction loses its importance. The human mind, created to worship, will attach itself to whatever performs the familiar pattern of power. Egypt's magicians understood this; modern culture has perfected it. Platforms, voices, and movements compete for belief through performance The serpent knows that if he can capture your attention, he can cultivate your allegiance.

Psychology calls this **social conditioning.** The more often an image, phrase, or behavior is repeated, the more authority it gains in the subconscious. This is why spiritual counterfeit functions the same way. When false systems echo Holy language long enough, they inherit unearned credibility. The enemy does not need to destroy reverence for God; he only needs to disrupt the focus among the counterfeits.

This is why the first miracle in Mose's ministry was not water from a rock or manna from heaven—it was the swallowing of serpents. God demonstrated that His authority does not compete; it consumes we are called to walk in dominion in the earth. You are only able to walk in this authority when you are operating in obedience. Aaron's rod devoured the magician's rods to teach every generation that true power overpowers every false delusion. God's works do not need approval, it defines reality.

"But Aaron's rod swallowed up their rods."
— Exodus 7:12 KJV

In our time, imitation has taken new forms. It speaks through polished language, curated images, and emotional performance.

The world has learned to mimic sincerity, brand spirituality, to market compassion and merchandise people.

Yet the same law applies what is born of God carries substance; what is manufactured carries no real weight. The counterfeit always requires constant performance to maintain credibility, but true authority flows effortlessly from God's presence and the power of the Holy Spirit it comes naturally.

Believers must understand that imitation is not only external. It also operates within the mind whenever we replace revelation with ritualistic practices.

The serpent whispers, "Do what has always worked; say what people expect," until creativity is replaced by conformity.

The Holy Spirit, however, leads into newness—fresh obedience that cannot be mimicked because it is anchored in an ongoing relationship.

This is the difference between performance and purpose.

The mechanics of imitation rely on three invisible levers:

1. **Recognition:** The mind finds comfort in what it identifies as familiar, and the deceiver leverages that recognition to lower critical evaluation.

2. **Consistency:** Repeated exposure builds a false sense of reliability, when something is consistently presented, it begins to seem inherently credible.

3. **Validation:** Imitation validates one's sense of worth. It convinces both parties that resemblance signals shared status and value.

The modern church, like ancient Egypt, must decide whether to live by the trap of the strategy or by submission. A generation conditioned by visual proof will always struggle with invisible authority. We must be people of faith without it we cannot please God. Yet authority and faith remain the measure heaven recognizes. The serpent can mimic miracles, but he cannot mimic meekness. He can imitate movement and trick you to operate with the wrong motive. He can reproduce sound, but not Holy Spirit.

"There is a way which seemeth right unto a man, but the end thereof are the ways of death."
— Proverbs 14:12 KJV

The appearance of rightness is the serpent's favorite disguise. It offers logic without lordship, excitement without endurance. This is why God trains His people to discern beneath the surface.

Every act must be tested for its origin.

The Holy Spirit teaches us to ask, does this produce surrender or self?

Does it draw me closer to obedience or to validation? True authority always restores order; imitation multiplies confusion that lead to disobedience.

The confrontation in Egypt was more than an ancient history story. It was a prophecy about how every generation would face the tension between what is displayed and what is hidden beneath the surface. We need to understand God allows imitation to manifest so that discernment can mature. The believer who recognizes a resemblance without revelation has already begun to walk in spiritual intelligence. Imitation is recognizable; walking in this type of authority is real power. Imitation copies patterns, authority births them through authenticity. Imitation impresses crowds, authority transforms hearts to bring real change. The difference is one exhausts the performer; the other empowers the obedient and gains strength. This is why the mind that understands this will never again confuse the appearance of truth with authenticity.

The Psychology of Deception

If imitation begins outside of humanity, then deception completes its work inside. The serpent's greatest tool is not power; he knows he cannot have ultimate power; it is persuasion. He studies how the human mind forms conclusions and then learns to interrupt the process between revelation and response.

In Eden he did not create doubt from nothing, he simply *redirected* Eve's reasoning a manipulation tactic that allowed her to begin to doubt the truth.

"Now the serpent was more subtil than any beast of the field which the LORD God had made. And he said unto the woman, Yea, hath God said, Ye shall not eat of every tree of the garden?"
— ***Genesis 3:1 KJV***

With one question he shifted her focus from **trust** to **interpretation**. When the mind begins to interpret before it obeys, deception has already entered. God's commands were meant to be received in faith, not negotiated through curiosity or your own understanding.

Our desire must be in line with God's will for our life.

Modern psychology calls this ***cognitive dissonance***: the discomfort that occurs when conviction and desire collide. The serpent leverages this discomfort. He invites the believer to relieve tension by altering truth rather than submitting to it.

Eve's reasoning was simple—if the fruit looks good, feels desirable, and promises insight, it must not be wrong. The logic was sound; the loyalty was misplaced. Deception always begins as justified rebellion.

"And when the woman saw that the tree was good for food, and that it was pleasant to the eyes, and a tree to be desired to make one wise, she took of the fruit thereof, and did eat."
— ***Genesis 3:6 KJV***

The sequence has never changed:

1. **Observation** – *She saw the tree.*
2. **Interpretation** – *It was pleasant to the eyes.*
3. **Rationalization** – *It was desired to make one wise.*
4. **Action** – *She took and did eat.*

This is the psychological pattern of deception: *Stimulus → Evaluation → Justification → Participation.*
Every sin, every compromise, still follows this order.

The enemy knows that reasoning feels righteous when it is emotionally satisfying. This is why many believers' mistake *agreement* for *discernment.* The heart says, "This feels right," and the mind baptizes the feeling as truth. Scripture warns,

"The heart is deceitful above all things, and desperately wicked: who can know it?"
— Jeremiah 17:9 KJV

This is what **1 John 2:16** describes as "all that is in the world" is not merely external influence—it is a mirror of what resides within fallen human nature. The lust of the flesh, the lust of the eyes, and the pride of life are not introduced by the world; they are activated by it. The world system does not create desire, it reveals and amplifies what already exists within the human heart.

This is why Scripture does not only warn us about what surrounds us, but what operates within us.

When the text declares "all that is in the world," it is not speaking only of systems, culture, or environment—it is describing the internal architecture that responds to those systems.

The serpent's approach has always depended on this reality: he does not need to manufacture new desires; he only needs to redirect existing ones.

This is why Jesus in **John 2 24-25** *"did not commit himself unto them...* for he knew what was in man."

He did not respond to outward expression alone—He discerned the inward condition. He understood that the behavior pattern is not the origin of deception, but the result of internal agreement. What is in man determines how man interprets what is around him.

The lust of the flesh appeals to appetite.
The lust of the eyes appeals to perception.
The pride of life appeals to identity.

Together, they form the three entry points through which deception interacts with human psychology.

This is the same structure seen in Eden.
This is the same structure seen in the wilderness with Christ.
And this is the same structure that continues to operate within every system that seeks to influence the mind today.

The world presents the catalyst, but the response is determined by what is already within. This is why the transformation must begin internally. Let the word be your guide to freedom, considering what is not healed within will always be activated from without.

This is the craftiness of the patterns the serpent studies, but those patterns are rooted in internal tendencies. He observes reactions, and those reactions are driven by deeper structures within the heart and mind.

This is why Christ did not trust external agreement—He discerned internal condition.

This is why renewal of the mind is not optional—it is essential for life survival.

You must realize until what is "in man" is transformed, what is "in the world" will always find agreement.

Emotion is a poor compass when the spirit is untrained. Feelings respond to what is immediate; discernment responds to what is eternal. The serpent manipulates the emotion to create an urgency that drowns self-examination. He did it with Eve in a garden; he does it now through screens and stages—wherever speed replaces stillness.

The Psychology of Repetition

Deception also works through weariness. When the mind is overwhelmed by fatigue illusion, this is where you become exhausted. Then you begin to accept the reoccurrence as reality. Pharaoh's magicians repeated their enchantments; Israel's false prophets repeated false hope; today's systems repeat slogans until conviction sounds intolerant. The enemy does not need to prove falsehood; he only needs to make truth mentally draining.

"For the time will come when they will not endure sound doctrine; but after their own lusts shall they heap to themselves teachers, having itching ears."
— 2 Timothy 4:3 KJV

The phrase *"itching ears"* describes curiosity divorced from commitment. It is the mental craving for stimulation rather than sanctification. The believer begins to collect voices instead of submitting to one Shepherd who will never leave you astray.

John 10:11-18. This is how deception matures, exposure without obedience.

Psychologists note that repeated stimulation without rest produces *desensitization*—the numbing of response. Spiritually, it becomes indifference. People no longer deny God; they simply stop reacting to Him. Pharaoh's heart hardened not just through hatred, however through habit the way he thought.

This was a lesson taught through the generations that came before him that followed man and not God a traditional way of thinking.

The Deceptive Reward System

The world rewards imitation with visibility influencing. It celebrates persuasion more than purity. Social hierarchies form around charisma, not conviction. This collective psychology is the serpent's masterpiece: a civilization that confuses applause for anointing.

Consider Balaam. He heard God clearly but returned to the same question because the offer of wealth appealed to his insecurity.

"And God came unto Balaam at night, and said unto him, If the men come to call thee, rise up, and go with them; but yet the word which I shall say unto thee, that shalt thou do."
— Numbers 22:20 KJV

God permitted movement but restricted the message. Balaam's mind, however, equated permission with approval.

That is the psychology of compromise: when your patience feels like permission, the heart assumes change in command.

The serpent convinces one that delayed consequence equal's divine consent. In the New Testament, Simon the sorcerer exposed the same thought pattern. He believed the gospel's power could be purchased. His mindset was not rebellion but *misidentification.* He saw the Holy Spirit as a marketable force, not a governing Presence. This is the strategy in the world today prostituting the word of God for personal gain, saying God say and he did not.

"Thy heart is not right in the sight of God."
— Acts 8:21 KJV

Both men illustrate the same principle: deception distorts motive before it alters the message. It begins by shaping the internal reward system—what the mind defines as success and wealth.

The serpent's question is never "Do you believe in God?" It is "What do you believe God values most?" If we answer incorrectly, we can serve Him publicly while opposing Him mentally.

The Emotional Architecture of Deception

The enemy constructs deception in layers:

1. **Flattery** – convinces you that understanding equals obedience. Imitation appeals to ego. It convinces both the deceiver and the deceived that similarity equals equality.
2. **Fear** – Whispers that obedience will cost too much. This brings anxiety It is also a response rooted in a perceived threat that, when misaligned with truth, distorts perception and influences decision-making.
3. **Fatigue** – dulls the will until delay feels safe. This brings on a state of depletion where endurance declines and discernment become more vulnerable to compromise.
4. **Familiarity** – normalizes the compromise until conviction disappears. The mind relaxes around what it recognizes. The serpent uses familiarity to lower discernment.

   By the time the final layer settles, the believer no longer senses danger. This is why Jesus said,

"Take heed therefore that the light which is in thee be not darkness."
— Luke 11:35 KJV

He was speaking about perception—the faculty of inner evaluation. Darkness disguised as light is deception perfected.

In practical terms, deception today appears whenever influence outweighs intimacy, whenever metrics outweigh ministry, whenever convenience outweighs conviction. The serpent no longer hides behind stone idols; he hides behind platforms of status.

Yet psychology remains identical, admiration without accountability.

The antidote begins with awareness. As believers we must learn to slow the sequence. Before reacting, reflecting, before agreeing, discerning. This interrupts the serpent's rhythm. The Spirit of truth reclaims the space between thought and choice. In that pause, obedience can breathe again.

Environment is a primary factor in conditioning; each country and state operates within systems that influence how people think, respond, and form patterns.

The Psycho-Demography of Control

If psychology explains how an individual is deceived, psycho-demography reveals how *entire populations* can be trained to think in ways that serve a system rather than their Creator.
Pharaoh did not simply enslave people with chains, he shaped their consciousness. His empire taught the Hebrews that value equals labor, that worth is measured in output. Centuries later Babylon would teach that value equals knowledge, and Rome would teach that value equals citizenship. Each civilization replaced divine identity with systemic utility.

"Be not conformed to this world: but be ye transformed by the renewing of your mind..."
— ***Romans 12:2 KJV***

The Greek word ***conformed*** means *to be pressed into an outward pattern.* Psycho-demography is that pressure applied on a mass scale. It operates through law, economy, media, and ritual, all working to make independent thought seem dangerous.

The serpent's strategy is simple: shape the rhythm of a person until rebellion against heaven feels like normal life.

Cultural Conditioning

Every generation absorbs its worldview through repetition and reward. Egypt used monuments and festivals; modern culture uses screens and slogans. Both function as memory devices—visual sermons preaching the same creed: *"You are self-made."* When that idea dominates, dependence on God appears primitive. Psychologically this creates *collective reinforcement.* The more voices repeat a belief, the less the individual tests it. Spiritually, it becomes *agreement without alignment*—a nation confessing faith in God while living by Pharaoh's calendar.

Egypt structured time through visible cycles that reinforced identity and worship:

- Nile flood seasons (Akhet) survival tied to controlled natural cycles
- Harvest festivals — provision attributed to false gods
- Temple rituals — daily repetition shaping devotion
- Pharaoh coronations — human authority reinforced as divine
- Seasonal offerings — allegiance repeated through ritual

Today, those same structures exist in different forms, shaping thought through modern systems:

- Work weeks — identity tied to productivity
- Pay cycles — value measured through income
- Consumer holidays — desire shaped through consumption
- Social media rhythms — attention trained daily
- Cultural seasons — identity influenced through trends

The structure has not changed—only the form. Time is still being used to train thought, and whatever consistently fills time eventually shapes identity.

Psycho-demography thrives wherever truth becomes statistical. If enough people approve of something, it feels morally correct.

This is why crowds cried *"Hosanna"* one week and *"Crucify him"* the next; social rhythm replaced spiritual revelation. The crowd had been trained to respond to the constructed display, not to the Spirit of God.

"For they loved the praise of men more than the praise of God."
— John 12:43 KJV

Modern Systems of Control

Today the same structure operates through digital conformity. Algorithms study your behavior the way Pharaoh studied the slaves. They learn what excites, divides, or frightens a population and feed it back until reaction becomes reflex.

That is psycho-demography in real time, predictive control through patterned exposure.

Believers today must see that such systems are not merely technical; they are theological. They compete for worship, demanding attention—the modern form of incense. Each clickbait is a bow; each share a small confession of allegiance. The serpent no longer whispers from a tree; he curates the feed.

The answer is not withdrawal, but discernment is key.

The renewed mind participates in culture without being patterned by it. Jesus prayed, *"I pray not that thou shouldest take them out of the world, but that thou shouldest keep them from the evil."*

(John 17:15 KJV). Separation now begins in understanding.

Breaking the Collective Spell

When one believer renews their mind, an entire environment begins to shift. Israel's exodus started with a single confrontation between truth and delusion. Revival always begins with cognitive rebellion against accepted lies. The psycho-demography of heaven functions through testimony: every renewed life becomes data against darkness.

The world studies behavior to predict it; God studies hearts to transform them. This is why pharaoh counted bricks; God counts your hairs. One monitors labor, the other measures love. This contrast reveals the heart of divine authority: it personalizes what the world standardizes.

The Mind of Christ

If the world shapes thought through pressure, Christ reshapes it through his presence. He does not demand conformity; He invites transformation. Paul writes,

"Let this mind be in you, which was also in Christ Jesus:
Who, being in the form of God, thought it not robbery to be equal with God:
But made himself of no reputation, and took upon him the form of a servant..."
— Philippians 2:5-7 KJV

This passage describes the divine psychology of humility. Jesus possessed absolute power yet refused to use it for validation. Where the serpent tempts humanity to prove, Christ teaches us to rest. Humility is not weakness; it is disciplined perception—the ability to view self through God's truth rather than through public reaction.

The Cognitive Structure of Christ's Authority

Christ's thinking followed a consistent pattern:

1. **Identity before activity.** At His baptism the Father declared, *"This is my beloved Son."* Only after that affirmation did ministry begin. The serpent reverses the order, urging people to achieve it before they believe.
2. **Obedience before understanding.** In Gethsemane He prayed, *"Nevertheless not my will, but thine, be done."* Emotion bowed to revelation. This reorders the human hierarchy: spirit leading, soul following, body serving.
3. **Service before status.** He washed feet to dismantle ambition's architecture. True authority manifests through voluntary limitation.

Psychologically this means stability under stress. The mind of Christ integrates emotion and reason beneath obedience, producing peace that circumstances cannot rewrite.

"Thou wilt keep him in perfect peace, whose mind is stayed on thee: because he trusteth in thee."
— ***Isaiah 26:3 KJV***

Peace is not the absence of pressure; it is the alignment of perception. The believer who internalizes Christ's structure becomes not easily traced to the enemy. The serpent can analyze habits but not holiness. Holiness interrupts the pattern.

Reprogramming the Inner Life

Renewal of the mind is **spiritual neuroplasticity**, the creation of new thought pathways through the discipline of truth. Meditation on Scripture rewires reaction; obedience reinforces it. Over time the believer's automatic response to temptation becomes submission rather than curiosity. That is the evidence of transformation.

'Sanctify them through thy truth: thy word is truth."

—John 17:17 KJV

The world trains through habitual cycles of lies; God trains through continuous revelation. Each verse memorized, each quiet act of surrender, is a small rebellion against the empire of counterfeit's a part of the kingdom of darkness.

Christ and Modern Pressure

In a culture obsessed with display, Jesus remains the model of divine restraint. He refused to perform on demand—before Herod, before the crowds, even before the cross. He understood that demonstration without direction feeds deception. His miracles always served revelation: sight that exposed sin, bread that exposed hunger of heart. To have the mind of Christ is to interpret every opportunity through obedience, not outcome we walk by faith. It is to measure success by faithfulness, not applause or approval. It is to stand in a world drunk on visibility and quietly embody truth that needs no advertisement.

"For the kingdom of God is not in word, but in power."
— 1 Corinthians 4:20 KJV

That power is the stability of a renewed mind.

Practical Discernment

The renewed mind is not mystical; it is measurable. Discernment is the evidence that transformation has reached thought. Scripture calls it the ability to

"prove what is that good, and acceptable, and perfect, will of God."

— ***Romans 12:2 KJV***

The Spirit of truth never leaves a believer guessing. He trains them until perception is refined into revelation.

1. Discernment in Information

The modern world lives in permanent broadcast. Words, images, and opinions arrive faster than reflection can form. Pharaoh's magicians had rods; today's systems have algorithms. Both manufacture presentations to occupy attention. If the serpent can control your focus, he can guide your thoughts. Discernment begins by reclaiming attention as Holy Territory.

"Beloved, believe not every spirit, but try the spirits whether they are of God."
— ***1 John 4:1 KJV***

However, testing requires time and truth does not shout; it stands. As a believer you must learn to pause before reacting—to reading slowly, to listen prayerfully, to separate emotion from evidence.

The Holy Spirit will never rush the soul into confusion.

This takes practice and discipline. One day at a time Faith to Faith and Glory to Glory.

2. Discernment in Influence

Influence is strategic. In every age people have mistaken charisma for calling. Saul looked at the part; David carried the presence. The young prophet in 1 Kings 13 obeyed God until admiration overruled instruction. The older prophet's reputation felt safer than God's command. The pattern repeats whenever believers treat visibility as validation.

"To obey is better than sacrifice."
— 1 Samuel 15:22 KJV

Discernment asks not, *"Who said it?"* but *"Who sent it?"*

A voice may quote Scripture and still contradict the Spirit. True authority will always draw hearts toward obedience, never dependence on personality. The counterfeit creates followers; the authentic creates sons and daughters.

3. Discernment in Intimacy

Deception often travels through affection. Judas approached with a kiss. Relationships become gates of influence; whichever voice we love most shapes our logic. Emotional loyalty can silence spiritual warning. The serpent wrapped manipulation in empathy long before modern culture named it. He says, *"I understand you,"* before he says, *"Disobey."* Jesus loved deeply yet remained governed by the mission. When Peter tried to protect Him from the cross, Jesus discerned the spirit behind his concern.

"Get thee behind me, Satan: for thou savourest not the things that be of God, but those that be of men."
— Matthew 16:23 KJV

Love without alignment leads to compromise. Discernment guards compassion so that mercy never becomes manipulation.

(Read That Again)

"Be ye therefore wise as serpents, and harmless as doves."
*— **Matthew 10:16 KJV***

The Three Tests of Every Voice:

1. **Does it glorify God or self?**
2. **Does it produce surrender or pride?**
3. **Does it agree with Scripture or adjust it?**

Where any answer falters, deception has entered. The Holy Spirit never flatters the flesh He intends to crucify it. He will convict you until you surrender, but you must choose he will not force you.

The Discipline of Stillness

Discernment grows in silence. Elijah found God not in wind or fire but in a still small voice. The noise of imitation feeds on volume; authority feeds on clarity. Regular quiet dismantles deception's rhythm the sound is important. In stillness, motives surface; in noise, they hide. The believer who practices silence will never be easily seduced by presentation.

The Serpents Strategy Insight

The Pattern Broken

Every counterfeit system depends on predictability. The serpent's dominion is data: habits, fears, triggers, preferences. When the Holy Spirit renews a mind, the data becomes useless. Heaven creates unpredictability through obedience, bringing light to the hidden darkness.

The Lord is exposing the architecture of imitation in this generation. He is revealing how entire cultures have been hypnotized by their performance. Entertainment has replaced the encounter; images have replaced intimacy. Jesus identifies what is **dormant** as dead, but He does not leave it that way. He calls it forth into life, restoring the capacity to perceive, to understand, and to walk in truth.

What was once unrecognized is no longer hidden, this is why life in Him brings clarity where there was once limitation.

Most people today do not understand what he was talking about when he said,

"But Jesus said unto him, Follow me; and let the dead bury their dead."

— ***Matthew 8:22 KJV***

Yet the remnant God is raising will not compete with Egypt; they will **outlast** it. Their stability will become its judgment.

"For the LORD giveth wisdom: out of his mouth cometh knowledge and understanding."
— ***Proverbs 2:6 KJV***

The LORD's divine wisdom is Heaven's Psychological Warfare. Each renewed thought is a strike against the empire of illusion. When believers refuse to mirror trends, they dismantle powers. When they speak truth without anxiety, they break the rhythm of fear. Revival will not look like a catastrophe; it will look like minds at rest in revelation.

God's Strategy of Renewal

Expose imitation – He allows false systems to reveal their emptiness.

1. **Educate perception** – He teaches believers to interpret motive, not motion.
2. **Establish authority** – He builds inner stability that external power cannot counterfeit.

The pattern is destroyed when discernment becomes a delight. The renewed believer no longer survives deception; they study it, understand it, and dismantle it through peace.

"Study to shew thyself approved unto God, a workman that needeth not to be ashamed, rightly dividing the word of truth."
— 2 Timothy 2:15 KJV

"And ye shall know the truth, and the truth shall make you free."
— John 8:32 KJV

Freedom is not emotional, it is comprehension. It is not measured by how one feels, but by what one is able to discern and remain aligned with. Emotion shifts, but truth does not, and any freedom built on what shifts will eventually collapse under pressure. True freedom is established when the mind is no longer governed by comfort, but by what is true, regardless of what that truth requires.

The moment truth becomes loved more than comfort, deception loses its place. Not because deception disappears, but because it is no longer received. The serpent does not lose power through absence, but through the loss of agreement. When the mind no longer seeks what feels right, but what is right, the strategies that once worked no longer find access.

This is where the shift begins.

Because deception requires an audience, and once truth becomes the standard, that audience is no longer available. What once appealed now exposes itself. What once persuaded now falls apart under discernment. The same voice may still speak, but it no longer carries influence, because it no longer finds alignment within.

This is the future of the Church—not a people driven by emotion, reaction, or cultural language, but a people established in understanding. A person whose minds cannot be marketed, because they are not influenced by persuasion. A people whose worship cannot be weaponized, because it is not rooted in performance, but in truth. A people whose obedience cannot be predicted, because it is not governed by external pressure, but by internal alignment with Christ. The stage of this generation has already been set, and what is being presented is constant. The language may change, but the pattern remains the same. What the world defines as awareness, many accept as truth, but recognition without alignment does not produce transformation. To see something is not the same as being established in what is true about it. Only those who are truly alive will discern the difference.

"I am crucified with Christ: nevertheless I live; yet not I, but Christ liveth in me: and the life which I now live in the flesh I live by the faith of the Son of God, who loved me, and gave himself for me."
— Galatians 2:20 (KJV)

This is not a statement of belief—it is a statement of identity.

To be crucified with Christ is not symbolic language; it is the end of self-governance. It is the removal of personal authority as the final voice. What remains is not a version of self-improved, but a life governed by Christ within. And where Christ governs, deception cannot lead, because there is no longer a self to appeal to in the same way. This is why the questions that follow are not casual, they are necessary. Most often what leads you will form you, and what forms you will determine your outcome.

Ask yourself:

What is leading me right now?
Not what I claim, but what I follow. Not what I say I believe, but what actually directs my decisions, my responses, and my patterns.

Have I truly surrendered to Christ?
Not in word, but in authority. Not in moments, but in governance. Is my life directed by Him, or do I return to myself when it becomes uncomfortable?

Does the path I am on lead to life or death?
Not where it begins, but where it ends. Not what it promises, but what it produces. Because every path has a direction, and every direction has an outcome.

These are not questions to answer quickly. They expose what is real.

Because freedom is not declared, it is demonstrated by what no longer has influence over you.

And where Christ truly governs, there is no divided authority.

PRAYER

The Renewed Mind

Father,
I come before You to yield every thought, every perception and perspective, every hidden motive.
Where delusion and lies have shaped me, dismantle it at the root.
Where fear has trained my decisions, deliver me.
Wash the habits of this world from my reasoning.
Teach me to recognize Your whisper above every distractions.

Let Your Word rebuild the architecture of my mind.
Sanctify the patterns of my thinking until obedience feels natural and rebellion feels foreign.
Heal the memories that have taught me false lessons.
Restore holiness without compromise, passion without pride, and confidence without control.

I renounce the flattery of imitation and the fatigue of performance. I receive the stability of Your peace.
Holy Spirit, interrupt my reflexes with revelation; replace reaction with reflection.
When I am tempted to prove, remind me to abide.

When I am pressured to imitate, remind me I already belong.

In Jesus name,

Amen

PROPHETIC DECREE

I decree that every counterfeit pattern in my life collapses under the weight of truth.
I am not a reflection of this age; I am an expression of Heaven.
Imitation loses its influence; authenticity becomes my language.

My thoughts are governed by the Spirit of God.
My emotions serve revelation, not reaction.
My discernment cuts through confusion like light through fog.

I carry authority that cannot be purchased, your presence that cannot be copied, peace that cannot be provoked.
The psychology of the world no longer predicts my behavior; the wisdom of Christ determines it.

I will walk through cultures of deception untouched, carrying clarity wherever I go. Systems of control lose their grip when

I enter the room, for the Kingdom of God within me is greater than every imitation around me.

I decree renewal over my mind, my household, my generation.
The serpent's strategy is exposed and dismantled burned by the fire of God, and the mind of Christ prevails.

So it is, and so it shall remain.

In Jesus name,

Amen

CHAPTER FIVE

HOW SYSTEMS REWIRE ALLEGIANCE

The most enduring systems in Scripture did not conquer visible power, they advanced through steady influence, shaping agreement over time. Perception forms first, gradually giving way to attachment, and attachment, if left unchallenged, develops into allegiance. What is encountered consistently becomes familiar.

Over time, what is accepted without understanding is no longer questioned, but absorbed until it forms identity itself.

What begins as exposure eventually becomes identity when it is repeated long enough without interruption.

The serpent in Eden introduced distortion through a single conversation, but what began in a moment was later refined into systems. Egypt, Sodom, and Babylon did not merely practice distortion—they structured it, embedding it into environments that trained the mind continuously. These were not merely sinful cities. They were immersive systems that rewired internal responses through repetition, exposure, and reinforcement over time.

Psychologically, the human mind adapts to its environment through exposure-based normalization. What is seen repeatedly lowers emotional resistance. What lowers resistance increases familiarity. Familiarity creates a sense of internal stability. Stability becomes preference, and preference, when reinforced, becomes allegiance. You must choose where your loyalty will be.

This is how allegiance shifts without conscious rebellion.
It does not begin with rejection of truth—it begins with gradual adjustment to an environment.

Egypt — Dependency Conditioning

Egypt did not only enslave bodies. It regulated survival itself, embedding control into the most basic human needs.

Pharaoh controlled agricultural cycles, food distribution, labor schedules, and ritual observances. Provision was not freely accessed; it was mediated through centralized authority. The system embedded survival into hierarchy, making dependence unavoidable.

When survival depends on the structure, the brain encodes safety around that structure. What provides becomes what is trusted, even when that provision exists within oppression.

This is why Israel remembered food before remembering oppression.

"We remember the fish, which we did eat in Egypt freely..."
— ***Numbers 11:5 KJV***

The memory is selective. Trauma and provision were both present, yet the mind preserved what stabilized it. Stability, even when rooted in bondage, becomes emotionally significant because it reduces uncertainty.

The brain prioritizes what feels consistent over what is actually free.

This is dependency conditioning.

Over time, repeated supply reduces the perceived need for trust in unseen provision. Egypt replaced daily reliance on God with controlled, visible mediation. What could be counted replaced what required faith.

When God removed Israel from Egypt, He did not merely remove chains, He dismantled dependency architecture.

The wilderness was not absent; it was recalibration.

The supply rhythm was intentionally disrupted. Manna was given daily, not stored permanently, forcing continual reliance rather than accumulated control.

"That I may prove them, whether they will walk in my law, or no."
— Exodus 16:4 KJV

The test was psychological. Would they reattach to secure structure, or anchor trust in covenant? Would they seek stability in what they could control, or in who God is?

Dependency systems create emotional loyalty, this is how they regulate survival. Once survival is linked to structure, departure does not feel like freedom, it feels like danger.

Sodom — Moral Desensitization Through Saturation

Sodom functioned differently. It did not regulate the supply; it normalized the inversion, reshaping moral boundaries through continuous exposure rather than structural dependency.

Repeated exposure to collective behavior reduces your internal alarm signals. What once produced real conviction begins to feel familiar, and what becomes familiar begins to feel acceptable. Neuroscience describes this as habituation. Scripture reveals it through progression.

"Lot pitched his tent toward Sodom."
— Genesis 13:12 KJV

Your orientation alters proximity. Proximity alters your perception. What you face, you eventually move toward, and what you move toward eventually shapes how you see. Peter writes,

"Vexed his righteous soul from day to day."
— 2 Peter 2:8 KJV

Day-to-day exposure reduces sensitivity. Desensitization does not immediately remove righteousness—it weakens its intensity. Your conviction becomes quieter, less urgent, less immediate.

Sodom's power was collective reinforcement. When many normalize what God forbids, then dissent becomes isolating, and isolation creates pressure to adapt. The mind begins to weigh, belonging to be truth against the conviction from the Holy Spirit.

Cultural saturation gradually reframes abnormal behavior as social stability. What was once resisted becomes tolerated, and what is tolerated long enough becomes integrated.

The psychological mechanism is social conformity pressure combined with repetition. The longer exposure continues, the less reactive the conscience becomes, not because truth has changed, but because sensitivity has been reduced.

This is not immediate corruption.
It is **progressive recalibration.**

Recalibration is the gradual adjustment of internal standards through repeated exposure. The mind does not abandon truth all at once; it shifts its sensitivity into small, almost unnoticeable increments. What once produced conviction begins to produce tolerance. What once felt wrong begins to feel distant. What once disturbed the conscience begins to settle into familiarity. This process is not loud, it is layered. Each exposure lowers resistance slightly. Each repetition softens reaction. Each moment of tolerance rewrites the boundary between what is accepted and what is rejected. Over time, the internal measure of right and wrong is not removed and it is adjusted.

This is **recalibration**. It is progressive on the grounds that it happens over time, not through a single decision, but through accumulated exposure. The mind is not forced to agree; it is trained to adapt.

The conscience is not silenced instantly; it is desensitized gradually until its voice becomes less urgent, less sharp, and easier to ignore.

The danger is not that truth disappears.
The danger is that it no longer feels immediate.

What once required resistance now requires awareness.
What once triggered conviction now requires discernment.

This is how environments reshape perception without demanding open rebellion. The individual does not feel like they have changed, given that each shift was small enough to feel reasonable. But over time, those small adjustments form a completely different internal alignment. This is why Lot remained in Sodom while his soul was still vexed. The external environment had not immediately erased righteousness, but it had begun to recalibrate its intensity. The tension remained, but the urgency weakened. Progressive recalibration does not remove light. It dims its contrast. And when contrast is reduced, clarity is compromised.

Babylon — Identity Reassignment and Cognitive Overlay

Babylon represents the most advanced conditioning system in Scripture, considering it did not only influence behavior, it redefined the identity at its core.

"Unto whom the prince of the eunuchs gave names."
— Daniel 1:7 KJV

Renaming is not symbolic only; it is a cognitive overlay. Identity language shapes self-perception, and self-perception shapes moral decision-making. What a person is called begins to influence how they see themselves, and how they see themselves determines how they live.

Babylon layered multiple systems of influence simultaneously:

• **Educational immersion**

Babylon did not begin with behavior—it began with learning. Education was not neutral; it was sensory overloading. The young captives were trained in the literature, philosophy, and knowledge systems of Babylon until their understanding of reality was filtered through a new framework. What they learned began to reshape how they interpreted everything they previously knew.

This is why you must be led and taught by the Spirit of God to understand what's hidden beneath. Education determines interpretation. When knowledge is received within a controlled system, it does not simply inform, it reorients one's perception. Over time, truth is not always rejected outright, it is reinterpreted through the lens of what has been repeatedly taught.

This is how immersion works; it surrounds the mind with a consistent narrative until the alternative perspectives feel foreign or unnecessary. Remember man tries to control the narrative, but the LORD, says "He is GOD". There is freedom in Him. The goal was not information; it was internal alignment with Babylon's way of thinking.

• **Linguistic alteration**

Language is not just communication—it is identity encoded in words. When Babylon changed their names, it was not cosmetic; it was psychological. Names carried meaning and meaning shaped the identity. We must remember the LORD changes names too…

To rename is to redefine. The original names of Daniel and the others reflected their relationship to God. The new names assigned by Babylon reflected allegiance to a different system. This created a cognitive tension between who they were and what they were being called. However, they knew who they were in God.

Language shapes internal dialogue.

Remember what a person is repeatedly called begins to influence how they think about themselves, and how they think about themselves determines how they act. Over time, if unchallenged, the external label begins to override internal identity.

This is how systems rewrite identity without removing the reminders, but by changing the language through which identity of them is processed.

• **Cultural reward systems**

Babylon did not force compliance, it incentivized it. Advancement, privilege, and access were given to those who aligned with the system. This created a reward structure where obedience to Babylon produced visible benefit.

Reward reinforces behavior.

When compliance produces elevation, the mind begins to associate alignment with success. Over time, the desire for that advancement can override the commitment to truth, although through gradual compromise this too leads to disobedience.

The system teaches: ***what benefits you must be right.***

This is where allegiance begins to shift slowly, not just through rejection of God, but through the attachment to what the system rewards. The individual does not feel like they are abandoning truth; they feel like they are progressing.

But progression within a misaligned system still leads you away from God.

• **Administrative advancement**

Babylon integrated captives into positions of influence, giving them roles within the very system that sought to reshape them. Authority was granted within the structure, creating a sense of belonging and responsibility tied to Babylon's operation.

Position creates attachment.

When a person is given influence within a system, their identity begins to intertwine with its function. Their success becomes linked to the system's success, and their responsibility reinforces their participation.

This is deeper than reward—it is **integration.**

The system no longer feels outward it feels personal. Leaving it no longer feels like a withdrawal, it feels like loss of purpose, position, and identity.

This is how allegiance becomes internalized. Not through twisting anyone's arm, but through participation that is done willing.

This incorporation operates through a reward-based reinforcement. Compliance produces this type of elevation, and elevation supports the attachment. What is rewarded is frequent, and continual which helps to become your identity. The serpent's strategy is cunning.

This is **identity conditioning**.

Over time, the mind begins filtering reality through the new structure. What once felt strange begins to feel integrated, not because it is true, but because it has been consistently reinforced. Daniel resisted because he anchored his identity internally, he already knew what was forbidden.

"But Daniel purposed in his heart..."
— Daniel 1:8 KJV

Without proper conviction, temptation does not feel like pressure. You can stay disciplined even in the center of the situation.

This is why the will must be surrendered to the Lord, so that life is governed by His authority rather than shaped by the surrounding systems of the world.

Babylon did not erase covenant history; it overlaid it with an alternative meaning. The original truth remained present, but its interpretation was gradually replaced.

Overlay produces an internal conflict.
Prolonged overlay produces a replacement.

Babylon did not remove their moral identity in a single moment; it layered it with new structures over until the original identity was no longer the dominant influence.

In today's society as believers, you must become disciplined in the word of God and ways of God to be able to withstand the principalities operating in the regions of the world today. We must be steadfast in our allegiance to the one and only Supreme ruler of our Kingdom. What kingdom you apart of is very important to live.

Shared Psychological Architecture

Egypt, Sodom, and Babylon differ structurally, yet they operate through the same internal mechanisms, revealing a consistent pattern of influence:

1. Habits lowers resistance
2. Reward increases attachment
3. Saturation reshapes identity
4. Stability becomes emotional loyalty

The result is **conditioned allegiance.**

Conditioned allegiance does not feel rebellious, it feels reasonable. It does not feel like and exit it feels like adaptation. It feels safe, most often if it has been cultivated in strengthen over time.

This is why deliverance often feels destabilizing. The removal of conditioning produces discomfort, and discomfort is often misinterpreted as danger brings awareness to your environment.

Israel longed for Egypt.
Lot hesitated leaving Sodom.
Captives adapted to Babylon.

Their atmosphere had reshaped their internal equilibrium.

Christ — The Counter-Conditioning

What systems build through cycles, Christ dismantles through mind renewal. He does not simply oppose structures he pulls them from the root. He reconstructs personalities internally, addressing every area in and through the earth that would alternate his principles from being established. True freedom is found only in Him

"If the Son therefore shall make you free, ye shall be free indeed."
— John 8:36 KJV

Freedom here is not optional it is determined by where one's devotion is truly aligned. It is not dependent on the environment; it is rooted in character building a solid foundation that will not move.

Where Egypt built dependency, Christ becomes provision.

"I am the bread of life."
— John 6:35 KJV

Where Sodom normalized a corrupted structure, Christ restores clarity.

"*Ye shall know the truth, and the truth shall make you free."*
— John 8:32 KJV

Where Babylon reassigned identity, Christ redefines it.

"If any man be in Christ, he is a new creature."
— 2 Corinthians 5:17 KJV

“*New creature*” is not a behavioral adjustment—it is an identity reconstruction without cultural assimilation.

The serpent’s systems reshape through exposure.
Christ restores through transformation.

“Be not conformed to this world: but be ye transformed by the renewing of your mind.”
— ***Romans 12:2 KJV***

Conformity is environmental imprinting.
Transformation is covenant realignment.

Christ does not merely remove people from systems; He rebuilds the internal architecture those systems once shaped.

“Set your affection on things above, not on things on the earth.”
— ***Colossians 3:2 KJV***

The atmosphere presses downward, shaping perception through patterns and pressure.
Christ reorients upward, restoring alignment through truth and identity.

Allegiance does not change through information alone.
It shifts when your identity through Christ is restored.

CHAPTER SIX

FAMILIAR SPIRITS & EMOTIONAL MEMORY

When Memory Feels Like Home

Every emotion leaves something behind, and what is felt does not simply pass when the moment ends, it settles into the mind and begins to shape how a person yields over time. What is remembered is not silent, it continues to influence how situations are understood, how reactions form, and what is expected to move forward.

The serpent understands that since people rarely return to something out of a desire for rebellion in its original state. They return to what feel familiar. Familiarity lowers resistance, and what is known can begin to feel secure, even when it is destructive and deadly. Over time, what is familiar becomes easier to accept, not on the basis of truth, but on the basis of experience.

Scripture reveals a deeper layer of what is taking place:

"For rebellion is as the sin of witchcraft, and stubbornness is as iniquity and idolatry."
— 1 Samuel 15:23 KJV

Witchcraft is not always expressed through ritual or spell craft; it is often manifested through control manipulation of the emotion.

Every time emotion governs obedience, something other than truth has taken authority this is where the deception is secretly hidden.

Familiar spirits exploit this reality by attaching themselves to memories, especially memories charged with strong emotional weight. They do not need to create new experiences; they replay existing ones. They bring back the sound, the scent, the image, the feeling, until the body begins to respond before the spirit has time to discern the deeper motives and intentions of the delusion.

Often the reaction becomes automatic. It feels like a natural response, it feels justified. Yet when a response is formed outside of truth it is no longer neutral it is being directed.

The world calls this conditioning. The Lord calls it discipline.

Memory, when left unexamined, does more than remind, it begins to guide without one realizing it. It carries weight through the experience, and that weight can influence how a person sees, reacts, and decides. This is where agreement forms, often without awareness, through what is continually accepted and not brought into alignment with truth.

So, the Spirit begins deliverance not only with forgiveness, but with renewal of memory. Forgiveness addresses the past; renewal addresses its influence.

Freedom is not forgetting—it is remembering differently.

"Forgetting those things which are behind, and reaching forth unto those things which are before."
— Philippians 3:13 KJV

"Forget" in Paul's Greek vocabulary does not mean erasing information—it means no longer being influenced by it. The memory may remain, but its authority is removed.

God does not erase the past; He rewrites its influence. He reinterprets what once governed you and removes its power to direct you and bring forth sanctification a process of renewal.

When revelation reinterprets memory, familiar spirits lose territory.

Familiar spirits operate through recognition rather than introduction. Their access point is not unfamiliar patterns, but history, what has already been experienced, felt, and internalized. The term *"familiar"* points to intimacy of awareness. These spirits function within patterns that have already been established, engaging the individual through what is known rather than what is new.

"Regard not them that have familiar spirits..."
— Leviticus 19:31 KJV

To regard means to give attention, to incline the mind toward something, allowing it to remain in focus. This shows that their influence is sustained through engagement. What has already taken shape in thought becomes the point of access, and attention keeps that access active.

"And the soul that turneth after such as have familiar spirits..."
— Leviticus 20:6 KJV

Turning describes movement that begins within. Before anything is acted out, there is already alignment forming in interest, curiosity or reflection. This is where their activity is rooted, in the inward life before one responds in their action.

They function by aligning with existing internal structures:

- emotional memory
- learned responses
- unresolved experiences
- internal narratives

What has been formed internally becomes the environment they move within.

"Be sober, be vigilant..."
— 1 Peter 5:8 KJV

Vigilance speaks to awareness, not just of what is happening around you. Over time, patterns reveal themselves through consistency. Certain thoughts return in similar moments.

Certain reactions surface in familiar ways. What once felt like a single experience begins to show itself as something ongoing.

This is where discernment becomes necessary.

Not every thought needs to be followed.
Not every reaction needs to be trusted.
Not everything that feels familiar is aligned with truth.

When something continues to surface in the same way, especially when it leads away from God's truth, it should be examined rather than accepted. Awareness allows a person to recognize when a response is being shaped by something that has already taken hold, rather than by what is true in the present.

Familiar spirits operate within that space of recognition. They do not need to force anything; they rely on what is already known being accepted without question. This spirit influence remains where it is not examined, and it weakens when it is brought into the light.

"Neither give place to the devil."
— Ephesians 4:27 KJV

Place refers to ground, space that permits influence. This ground is often an internal form where thought, emotion, and belief remain unaligned with truth.

Where alignment is absent, access remains.

"For as he thinketh in his heart, so is he."
— Proverbs 23:7 KJV

The heart, as the center of thought and perception, determines identity expression. When the internal agreement is established, it shapes a response without requiring outside pressure. This is why renewal is essential.

"When the unclean spirit is gone out of a man..."
— Matthew 12:43–45 KJV

Removal without transformation leaves the structure unchanged. If the internal framework remains intact, re-entry is possible because the environment has not been changed.

This is why familiar spirits persist where internal patterns remain the same.

"Submit yourselves therefore to God. Resist the devil, and he will flee from you."
— James 4:7 KJV

Submission precedes resistance. Authority is not exercised independently; it flows from a connection with God. Where the will is yielded, the entry point that once allowed access is revoked.

Familiar Spirits – The Counterfeit Comforters

Familiar spirits do not only influence through patterns, they also imitate comfort. They present themselves in a way that feels understanding, drawing a person back into what has already been experienced, not to heal it, but to keep it active. They always want access. This is why recognizing and eliminating all access is very important. What makes this deceptive is that it does not always feel harmful. It can feel like reflection, remembering, even like processing. But instead of bringing clarity, it keeps a person connected to what has already shaped their responses.

This term can be called dysfunctional cycles; this is where the difference between sources must be understood.

"But the Comforter, which is the Holy Ghost... shall teach you all things, and bring all things to your remembrance..."

— John 14:26 KJV

The Holy Spirit brings truth, clarity, and direction. Familiar spirits bring what has already been, presenting it in a way that keeps a person connected to it without transformation.

One leads forward with transformation, bringing new life.
The other keeps a person cycling through what has already been bringing no life, which leads to a dead place. Familiar spirits feel comforting because they help reproduce understanding.

They present themselves as empathy, but their purpose is to containment. They hide themselves while appearing to connect.

They suggest that healing will cost identity, that letting go will remove something essential. But the Comforter does not numb the pain. He transforms it that you may become free to live life as the Lord intended...

"Blessed be God... who comforteth us... that we may be able to comfort them..."
— 2 Corinthians 1:3-4 KJV

What is healed becomes your victory. What is restored becomes a testimony. Where familiar spirits use one memory for control, God uses memory for purpose.

The process of breaking their influence follows a precise order:

1. Recognition of Pattern

What remains unidentified remains active. Familiar spirits operate through repeated internal pathways thought patterns, emotional triggers, and behavioral cycles that have become normalized over time. These are not isolated moments; they are structured responses.

Clarity exposes what habits are concealed.

"Let us search and try our ways..."
— Lamentations 3:40 KJV

This is not examination for condemnation, but for alignment. The purpose is clarity. Where a response repeats, there is a system sustaining it.We must have the Holy Spirit to navigate through it.

Exposure reveals the access point.

2. Removal of Agreement

Influence remains only where it is internally permitted. Agreement is not always verbal; it is often emotional or mental connections with what is contrary to truth.

"Neither give place to the devil."
— ***Ephesians 4:27 KJV***

To remove agreement is to withdraw consent. It is a decision at the level of the will that closes what previously was allowed.

Where agreement ends, access weakens.

---

3. Renewal of Thought

Patterns are continued through internal structure. Without renewal of the mind, removal is temporary.

"Be ye transformed by the renewing of your mind."
— ***Romans 12:2 KJV***

This replaces the old framework that once supported the pattern. It is just information it is reformation of perception.

What is consistently aligned with truth becomes the new reference point. A new structure replaces the old.

4. Reassignment of Emotional Response

Transformation becomes evident in reaction. If the same trigger produces the same response, the pattern remains intact. Emotional reactions must be brought under authority rather than left under the influence of memory or conditioning. This takes discipline by studying the word to bring forth divine alignment.

"Bringing into captivity every thought to the obedience of Christ."
— 2 Corinthians 10:5 KJV

Captivity is intentional redirection; a different response establishes a different pathway.

---

5. Establishment of New Alignment

What is removed must be replaced. Empty structure invites the return; a renewed structure prevents it.

"Walk in the Spirit, and ye shall not fulfil the lust of the flesh."
— Galatians 5:16 KJV

Walking indicates continuity. As alignment with the Holy Spirit becomes consistent, previous pathways lose power. What is no longer used is no longer continued. Familiar spirits do not remain because they are strong, they remain because patterns are still accessible, this means surrender has often not taken place.

When alignment shifts, structure changes.
When structure changes, access closes.
When access closes, influence ends.

Freedom is no longer something you reach, it is what you now walk in. This is not a temporary shift but an established way of being. You are no longer reacting to what once controlled you, you are moving with intention, grounded, aware, and fully aligned. What has been broken no longer defines you, and what has been established now sustains you.

Engrams – The Brain's Spiritual Blueprints

Psychologists use the word ***engram*** to describe the pattern the brain forms whenever experience and emotion fuse together. It is the imprint left behind when something is felt deeply enough to be remembered repeatedly.

Spiritually, an engram is more than a memory trace, it is pattern carrying authority. It does not wait for a conscious thought; it instructs the mind on how to feel before the thought has time to intervene. They are attached to negative emotional trauma.

"As he thinketh in his heart, so is he."
— Proverbs 23:7 KJV

When pain, pleasure, or fear occur repeatedly, the brain forms a pathway. That pathway becomes easier to travel each time it is used. Over time, response becomes automatic.

Demons study these paths. This is one of the great strategies the serpent uses.

They do not need to create new emotions, they move through existing ones, guiding the believer along familiar neurological routes that lead back to previous spiritual states. What has been felt before becomes the easiest place to return to.

Every addiction begins as an emotional engram.
Every cycle of fear, shame, or anger follows a path already formed by memory. That is why the serpent prefers the experience over an argument. If he can make you feel before you think, he bypasses resistance and gains influence without debate.

"The weapons of our warfare are not carnal, but mighty through God to the pulling down of strong holds; casting down imaginations."
— 2 Corinthians 10:4-5 KJV

Strongholds are fortified imaginations; engrams strengthened through repeated emotional agreement. They are not random thoughts; they are established internal structures.

They must be pulled down through new association, and truth joined with emotion. This is why worship heals.

When deliverance is experienced in your emotions, it is not only understood but felt, the brain begins to form new pathways. When God's love meets consciousness, what was once painful loses its control and you become whole.

This is why *"There is no fear in love; perfect love casts out fear: because fear hath torment. He that fearth is not made perfect in love. "**1 John 4:18 KJV***

God designed the system the enemy now attempts to misuse.

The human mind was created for meditation, for rehearsing truth until it becomes deeply ingrained into the mind. What is consistently meditated upon becomes a part of your inner life and this becomes natural.

Deliverance, then, is not only removing what bondage and spiritual danger can do, but also establishing what is right until it feels like freedom and believed to be true to walk in your calling. This is where continual prayer is needed to reclaim your foundation.

Emotional Loops – The Mind's Rehearsed Rebellion

An emotional loop is the soul's attempt to resolve what it never completed. It revisits the same internal state, seeking closure through the same similar experiences.

Unhealed emotion seeks resolution, so it recreates environments that resemble the original wound. This is why many believers find themselves in recurring patterns, different people, different situations, yet the same emotional outcome.

The faces change.
The pattern remains.

"The dog is turned to his own vomit again."
— 2 Peter 2:22 KJV

Peter's words describe a deep psychological reality: the mind returns to what feels familiar, even when it is harmful, because familiarity reduces uncertainty. What is known feels safer than what is unknown, even if what is known is destructive.

The serpent exploits this desire for familiarity.

He understands that the body seeks balance, and repeated emotional states—even unhealthy ones—create a form of chemical consistency. Over time, the brain begins to associate even negative experiences with a sense of stability. So, dysfunction becomes familiar, and familiarity begins to feel like comfort.

In Romans 7, Paul writes:

"For that which I do I allow not: for what I would, that do I not; but what I hate, that do I."
— ***Romans 7:15 KJV***

This is not only theological—it is psychological. Paul is describing the tension between a renewed spirit and programmed emotional pattern. His will is aligned with truth, but his internal patterns still reflect past conditioning. The conflict is not a lack of desire for righteousness—it is the presence of an established emotional pathway.

Every time the law of the mind wars against the law of the Spirit, emotion attempts to pull obedience back into what is habitual.

Emotional loops are broken when a new response is introduced.

When you respond differently—when you bless instead of reacting, when you worship instead of worrying—you interrupt the cycle. The pattern is disrupted, and a new pathway begins to form.

The serpent loses his expectation.
The cycle loses its connection.

"Walk in the Spirit, and ye shall not fulfil the lust of the flesh."
— Galatians 5:16 KJV

Walking implies ongoing action repeated movement in a new direction. God does not remove repetition; He redirects it.

He replaces destructive cycles with holy rhythms.

Each Spirit-led response becomes an interruption in what was previously established. Where the enemy anticipated a reaction, your obedience introduces the change.

Memory-Based Deception - How the Serpent Replays Emotion

Every deception begins with the remembrance of a thought.

The serpent's most effective weapon is not an argument, it is replay. He brings back what was felt, not just what was done. He presents memory in a way that distorts its meaning, so that conviction becomes confusing with nostalgia.

"When he speaketh a lie, he speaketh of his own: for he is a liar, and the father of it."
— John 8:44 KJV

The serpent's strategy can feel familiar carrying a greater influence than you are aware of. It aligns with what has already been experienced, the past. It does not feel strange, it feels comfortable, like a good fit.

That is why the serpent rarely creates entirely new temptations. He reintroduces previous ones with greater clarity, reinforcing them through history. He scripts temptation through perception.

When Eve looked upon the fruit, she was not only observing it, but she was also recalling the suggestion that had already been planted, *"Ye shall be as gods."* **(Genesis 3:5)**

The idea had already entered her mind. The image simply activated it bring into focus making it easier to agree with.

The thought became a pattern.
The memory became influence.
The influence became action.

Familiar spirits operate within this space. They function through recall. They revisit emotional experiences and present them in a way that encourages re-engagement. They do not demand, they suggest, using familiarity as their entry point.

"It wasn't that bad."
"You felt alive then."
"You were accepted there."

What begins as remembrance becomes negotiation.

This is why the Holy Spirit is called the Comforter.

"But the Comforter, which is the Holy Ghost... shall teach you all things, and bring all things to your remembrance..."
— John 14:26 KJV

He operates in the same space—memory—but with a different purpose. Where familiar spirits use memory to pull you backward, the Holy Spirit uses memory to move you forward. You must determine what voice you will respond to.

When the Holy Spirit brings it to memory, it carries revelation bringing new life. When deception brings it up to memory it is to torment, it carries the same pattern bringing death.

The difference is not the memory itself—it is the source and the direction it produces.

Healing Emotional Memory – How the Spirit Rewrites the Past

Emotional memory cannot be removed, but it can be redeemed. What has been experienced does not have to continue governing the response.

This truly must be the work of the Holy Spirit, **Surrender is Key.**

"He restoreth my soul."
— Psalm 23:3 KJV

To restore means to bring back into alignment. The Lord does not erase the past—He corrects its interpretation. When the Holy Spirit enters memory, He separates the event from the lie attached to it. The experience remains, but the false meaning is removed.

This is **Redemption….**

Pain once said, "You are unworthy."
Truth now says, "You were chosen."

Rejection once said, "You are alone."
Truth now says, "I was present with you."

Healing is not the absence of the memory—it is the removal of its authority over your life.

"And ye shall know the truth, and the truth shall make you free."
— John 8:32 KJV

Truth does not change what happened, it changes what it means. **Remember That…** Once the meaning is restored, the influence is broken. What once controlled your life no longer directs it. Inner healing is not optional, it is warfare. As long as emotional memory remains unhealed, it continues to provide access points. When truth is applied, those access points close. Leave no room for the enemy.

"Be renewed in the spirit of your mind."
— Ephesians 4:23 KJV

This type of renewal is not informational, it is relational. It occurs where truth and experience meet. Each time truth meets emotion, alignment is restored.

PRAYER

Father,
I surrender my memories to Your mercy.
Where pain speaks louder than your promises, let your truth interrupt the echo.
Where trauma has built reflexes, rebuild me through revelation.

I renounce every familiar spirit that feeds on my history.
I close every gate opened through nostalgia and regret.

Holy Spirit, enter every place of memory and redefine it through Your Word.
Teach me to feel without following, memories dictate and to remember without reliving the past.

Restore my soul until peace becomes my default.

In Jesus name, Amen.

PROPHETIC DECREE

I decree that my past no longer governs my perception.
My emotions serve truth; my memories serve my destiny.

Familiar spirits lose their access, and the Comforter reigns within me.

Every engram is rewritten through revelation.
Every cycle becomes instruction; every wound becomes wisdom.

I live from a healed memory, not from a repeated memory.

My mind is renewed, my emotions are sanctified, and my soul is restored.

I Am Redeemed in Jesus name……

CHAPTER SEVEN

The Queen of Heaven System:

Emotional Idolatry and Spiritual Witchcraft

Systems of Seduction – Definition and Origin

Definition of System:
A system is a structure of interdependent parts working toward a unified outcome, where each component reinforces the function of the whole. Spiritually, a demonic system is an organized strategy designed to produce rebellion through a very skilled and defined structure rather than disarray. These are not accidental enticements, they govern deception, structured in a way that influences the thought, emotion, and behavior over time, quietly bringing a snare to the soul. This spiritual *entrapment "Whoso pleaseth God shall escape from her; but the sinner shall be taken by her."*
— Ecclesiastes 7:26 KJV

Snare is often something that captures the soul through fear, desire, pride, emotional attachment, deception, or misplaced trust. What begins as an agreement can become bondage when discernment is rejected and truth is exchanged for comfort, validation, pleasure, or personal ambition. The enemy rarely approaches with chains first; he approaches through persuasion, familiarity, pressure, and gradual compromise until the mind becomes entangled before the person recognizes they are bound.

• *"The fear of man bringeth a snare..."* — ***Proverbs 29:25 KJV***
• *"Our soul is escaped as a bird out of the snare of the fowlers..."* —
Psalm 124:7 KJV

As a believer learn and acknowledge the dangers of continual recklessness behaviors that would keep you from developing a genuine relationship with Jesus, remove all distractions that bring any resistance to life, freedom is only through the Blood of Christ.

Definition of Seduction:
To seduce means to lead aside from truth through attraction, drawing the soul away without immediate resistance.
Seduction does not begin with rejection, it begins with lust, presenting an substitute that appears desirable enough to consider.
It suggests that what God promised can be obtained apart from the process He established, offering a outcome without obedience.

The serpent's first communication to Eve followed this pattern, seduction presented as enlightenment, questioning truth without directly opposing it.

"*Now the serpent was more cunning than any beast of the field which the Lord God had made.*
And he said unto the woman, Yea, hath God said...?"
— ***Genesis 3:1 KJV***

From Babylon forward, these type enticements developed into an organized system rather than isolated encounters. What began as a conversation became a structure embedded within culture, religion, and society.

The Queen of Heaven, recognized across generations as Ishtar, Astarte, Ashtoreth, Diana, and Semiramis, represented these organized reflections of seduction. Her system unified beauty, fertility, emotional influence, and symbolic power into a single framework that shaped entire civilizations.

Her worship extended beyond ritual; it influenced families, governed communities, and integrated into the economic and political structures. Temples functioned as centers of sensuality and sacrifice, where the affection was cultivated and directed to sustain loyalty. Those who served within her system did not simply lead worship; they managed the emotional environments that reinforced these devotions.

The people believed she governed the heavens, the cycles of the moon, the changing seasons, and fertility itself, and as a result, their internal responses were synchronized with what they believed she controlled. They refused to open there eyes to see this was idol worship, they were unaware they had moved for from the Lord.

"The children gather wood, and the fathers kindle the fire,
and the women knead their dough, to make cakes to the queen of heaven,
and to pour out drink offerings unto other gods,
that they may provoke me to anger."
— Jeremiah 7:18 KJV

Here, God reveals seduction not as an isolated act, but as a system embedded within daily life. The structure is generational—children, fathers, and mothers each participating, each reinforcing the same pattern they were taught from previous advisors.

What is repeated across generations becomes established as normal, and what becomes normal is rarely questioned.

The power of this system does not rest in visible witchcraft alone, but in disobedience that has been normalized to the point of acceptance. It teaches that emotion defines truth and that collective agreement validates the behavior. Once a family comes into this emotional agreement, their loyalty becomes stronger than the commitment to truth, and their conviction is treated as an attack against peace rather than an invitation to repentance and restoration.

Seduction does not present rebellion as opposition, it reframes it as relationship, gradually shifting perception until what once required repentance is replaced with reassurance. Compromise is reinterpreted as compassion, and bondage is presented as belonging.

The serpent's wisdom constructs comfort around what separates from God, until holiness is perceived as rules and regulations rather than a life-giving opportunity to live a blessed life.

In modern culture, this same structure operates through emotional religion and therapeutic idolatry. Influence is no longer confined to temples; it is distributed through platforms, screens, and constant exposure to things limiting the true manifestation of God's presence. Many are shaped more by opinion and affirmation than by love for Holy Scripture.

"Follow your heart" replaces *"Take up your cross."*
Worship is reshaped into performance, and conviction is treated as offense.

The throne of this system is rooted in the emotional center of man—the place where response is formed before reasoning is applied. Decisions are made internally before they are examined intellectually.

It does not require a denial of God; it requires that the emotion take priority over Truth.

"There is a way which seemeth right unto a man, but the end thereof are the ways of death."
— Proverbs 14:12 KJV

Every act of seduction begins with something that appears right. It carries logic because it is supported by your feelings, the internal response. Yet systems of seduction do not produce discernment; they create dependency on the system bring the delusion.

When peace becomes dependent on affirmation, the control shifts. Validation can then be used to guide your behavior, either withheld to produce instability or given to the direct desire the spirit of lust.

This system conditions believers to depend on an experience rather than obedience. Its modern altars are sustained through attention—recognition, approval, and continuous self-expression. This is where God's grace becomes sufficient, He gives us an opportunity to repent and move forward. Turn and Live….

Its messengers promote encouragement without correction.
Its atmosphere affirms without transforming.
Its doctrine suggests that happiness can exist without holiness.

But God's order remains unchanged.

"Thou shalt have no other gods before me."
— Exodus 20:3 KJV

He alone establishes the truth. When emotion is placed in authority, discernment is displaced. When an internal response becomes the standard, deception becomes the devotion, everyone must choose.

The result is **progressive desensitization.**

Over time, each generation inherits patterns that appear stable yet gradually separate them from the Covenant of God.

What is repeated becomes accepted, and what is accepted loses its ability to be challenged. Jeremiah witnessed this condition directly, the people continued in idolatry without understanding its burden.

"The Lord said, Seest thou not what they do in the cities of Judah and in the streets of Jerusalem?"
— Jeremiah 7:17 KJV

This question reveals divine grief. Perception had been altered. What was once visible as corruption was no longer recognized because reassurance had replaced clarity. When feelings govern, discernment weakens. When discernment weakens, perception becomes distorted. As a believer you must seek wisdom and develop good judgement this is commanded — ***Proverbs 4:5***

Psychological Insight

In neuroscience, emotional response precedes reasoning. Once the brain identifies something as desirable or threatening, thought processes often defend that response rather than evaluate it. Spiritually, the same pattern emerges when internal response is elevated above truth.

The cycle becomes self-reinforcing what is experienced repeatedly strengthens the belief, and what is believed reinforces continued the response.

God's Way

God restores order by reestablishing proper authority within the inner life.

The Holy Spirit leads.
The soul follows.
The body responds.

The truth becomes the foundation, and emotion is brought under its guidance. Emotion is not removed; it is redeemed and redirected.

"God is a Spirit: and they that worship him must worship him in spirit and in truth."
— John 4:24 KJV

We must understand true worship is not driven by revealing emotions. It is established through truth, sustained through obedience, and expressed through a genuine relationship.

It requires truth before articulation,
obedience before outward demonstration,
and revelation before movement.

This is where freedom begins, when emotion is no longer reigning and truth is restored to its rightful place.

Generational Worship — Jeremiah's Warning

Definition of Generational Worship:
Generational worship is the collective agreement of families to sustain a shared spiritual pattern, whether holy or corrupt, where continuity is preserved across time through repeated participation.

It is the emotional inheritance of belief systems in which obedience—or rebellion—becomes embedded within cultural identity and passed down as normal behavior rather than examined conviction.

In Jeremiah's time, this appeared as literal idol worship; today, it emerges through inherited mindsets—self-dependence, sensuality, unbelief, and emotional entitlement that are absorbed long before they are questioned.

"The children gather wood, and the fathers kindle the fire, and the women knead their dough, to make cakes to the queen of heaven, and to pour out drink offerings unto other gods, that they may provoke me to anger."
— Jeremiah 7:18 KJV

This passage reveals a fully developed system of idolatry functioning within the structure of family life.

Each member contributes—children provide resources, fathers initiate the ritual, and mothers prepare the offering. This is coordinated participation: rebellion practiced repeatedly until it resembles relationship. This is called *spiritual choreography* rebellion rehearsed until it feels like a relationship.

Their unity was not the problem—the direction of their unity was which was disobedience. What appears cohesive can still be corrupt when its foundation is misaligned with God 'truth. What God identifies as unity in rebellion, He defines as **provocation.**

Provocation is:

- intentional disregard for God's order
- repeated disobedience that becomes normalized
- choosing another system while still being aware of truth
- a pattern that invites divine response, not by accident, but by persistence

"Do they provoke me to anger? saith the LORD: do they not provoke themselves to the confusion of their own faces?"
— Jeremiah 7:19 KJV

The outcome of generational idolatry is distortion of identity.

The phrase "confusion of faces" in Hebrew points to disfigurement, loss of distinction, where clarity is replaced by mixture. When families elevate emotion above truth, definition begins to dissolve.

Boundaries between truth and tolerance become unclear.
Conviction is reinterpreted as cruelty.
Permissiveness is reframed as compassion.

The Queen of Heaven system operates by exchanging spiritual inheritance for emotional legacy. What should be transmitted through covenant is replaced by what is carried through reaction. Holiness is no longer cultivated; patterns are repeated. Reverence is no longer taught; responses are modeled.

The serpent does not need to persuade every generation individually if one generation can be conditioned effectively. What becomes familiar over time is eventually accepted without resistance, and what is accepted is rarely challenged.

Psychological Insight

In developmental psychology, children internalize parental responses—how authority is handled, how stress is processed, how affection is expressed.

These patterns form attachment structures that shape how individuals later relate to authority, intimacy, and correction.

Spiritually, this becomes a pattern of worship.

If comfort is consistently prioritized, then spiritual growth appears threatening. If affirmation is emphasized above correction, truth becomes negotiable. The Queen's system thrives where emotional consistency is valued more than moral clarity, since stability becomes defined by what is preserved, but not by what is genuine.

Scripture Connection

When Jeremiah confronted the people again years later, their response exposed how deeply this conditioning had taken root:

"Then *all the men which knew that their wives had burned incense unto other gods, and all the women that stood by, a great multitude, even all the people that dwelt in the land of Egypt, in Pathros, answered Jeremiah, saying,*

"As for the word that thou hast spoken unto us in the name of the LORD, we will not hearken unto thee."

"But we will certainly do whatsoever thing goeth forth out of our own mouth, to burn incense unto the queen of heaven... as we have done, we, and our fathers, our kings, and our princes... for then had we plenty of victuals, and were well, and saw no evil."

"But since we left off to burn incense to the queen of heaven, and to pour out drink offerings unto her, we have wanted all things and have been consumed by the sword and by the famine."
— **Jeremiah 44: 15-18 KJV**

Their reasoning reveals the psychological internal structure of rebellion. They associated provision with approval and relief with correctness. Their memory became the basis of their belief.

This is nostalgia used as justification.

They remembered the stability connected with disobedience, but ignored the consequences attached to it. Their conclusion was formed through experience, not through the truth of the gospel.

The queen's worship system had reconditioned their discernment until their emotional well-being was treated as evidence of divine favor.

Consequences of Generational Worship

1. **Economic Captivity** – "plenty of victuals" became their evidence of right standing. When provision changed, blame shifted toward God rather than toward their own disobedience.
2. **Spiritual Blindness** – "we saw no evil" reflects desensitization; perception became filtered through memory instead of truth.
3. **Intergenerational Agreement** – fathers, mothers, leaders, and rulers participated together, creating collective consent that gave the system authority to continue.

God's Way – Breaking the System

God sent Jeremiah not only to confront their behavior, but to expose the emotional reasoning sustaining it. The call to repentance addressed not just their actions, but their affections.

"Return, thou backsliding Israel, saith the LORD; and I will not cause mine anger to fall upon you: for I am merciful."
— Jeremiah 3:12 KJV

Repentance begins when direction changes internally.

The Hebrew word ***shuv*** (return) *means to turn back to reverse course at the level of the heart.*

Deliverance from generational worship requires reorientation, teaching the soul to value what it once resisted and release what it once depended on.

When Christ truly becomes Lord over one's life this is where captivity ends and liberation begin.

Modern Insight

This pattern continues in different forms:

- Families centered on success produce generations driven by achievement but lacking rest
- Households that prioritize security often produce fear-based decision-making
- Cultures that elevate image cultivate comparison and insecurity
- Churches that pursue performance create instability rather than transformation

These become modern altars social media, career, comfort, identity, and even ministry when it replaces true intimacy with God and replace with religious activity. Yet God continues to raise up voices who will be bold enough to call for "*return*" like Jeremiah, cried out, not against emotion itself, but against its authority Idol worship.

Holiness restores clarity.
Truth stabilizes the soul.

Revelation Insight

The Queen of Heaven does not simply gather worshippers—she trains families. She establishes patterns that become inherited, shaping perception until rebellion appears natural.

Her greatest success is convincing generations that they are governed by their emotions rather than responsible for them.

But the Spirit of Truth restores stewardship.

"For the LORD thy God is a consuming fire, even a jealous God."
— **Deuteronomy 4:24 KJV**

God's jealousy is not insecurity, it is protective, preserving relationship by removing what competes with it. His fire does not destroy identity; it consumes and refines it.

As a believer you must unlearn wrong behaviors taught by man and prior generations in their ignorance and relearn by allowing the correct teacher, the Holy Spirit to teach you truth.

"The Comforter, which is the Holy Ghost, whom the Father will send in my name, he shall teach you all things..."

— John 14:26 KJV.

This is where you allow the fire of God to cleanse you, bringing generational clarity, because *"our God is a consuming fire"* — **Hebrews 12:29 KJV,** and He *"shall sit as a refiner and purifier of silver"* — **Malachi 3:3 KJV,** removing what was formed outside of His will and restoring what aligns with His truth. We are born again into a different Kingdom, as it is written,

"My kingdom is not of this world"— **John 18:36 KJV;** therefore, *"if any man be in Christ, he is a new creature: old things are passed away; behold, all things are become new"*

— **2 Corinthians 5:17 KJV,**

"For He hath delivered us from the power of darkness, and hath translated us into the kingdom of his dear Son"

— Colossians 1:13 KJV

The Counterfeit Comforter –False Peace and Emotional Healing

Definition of Counterfeit Comfort:
Counterfeit comfort is any emotional relief that removes conviction without bringing renewal. It soothes pain while quietly sustaining bondage, allowing people to experience temporary ease while remaining internally unchanged. This is the queen of heaven's most effective ministry: to console rebellion in such a way that repentance never becomes necessary.

"For they have healed the hurt of the daughter of my people slightly, saying, Peace, peace; when there is no peace."
*— **Jeremiah 8:11 KJV***

The word *slightly* in Hebrew carries the meaning of something superficial treated on the surface but untouched at the root. It describes a wound that has been covered but not cleansed. The false prophets of Jeremiah's day offered *emotional anesthesia* instead of spiritual surgery. They understood what the people desired—to stop hurting—but failed to address what was required—to be healed. This is why the Queen's system exchanges truth for tranquility, the people accepted partial healing as if it was hope.

Revelation Insight

The queen of heaven spirit constructs environments of therapy while resisting repentance. It invites expression of pain but avoids surrender of it. It promotes vulnerability without accountability and substitutes validation for transformation, teaching that awareness alone equals deliverance. This is exactly what the serpent wants, to keep you in bondage on an emotional roller coaster. But God's peace is not an emotional state—it is the fruit produced by righteousness.

"*And the work of righteousness shall be peace; and the effect of righteousness quietness and assurance forever."*
*— **Isaiah 32:17 KJV***

Heaven's peace does not numb you it restores order. It does not accommodate rebellion; it transforms it. True peace is not experienced in avoidance but is established through obedience.

Psychological Insight

In modern psychology, emotional regulation without transformation of belief leads to ***suppression*** rather than healing. This is why so many generations before us and some still today are still controlled by her. When anxiety is managed but the underlying thought structure remains unchanged, the same patterns re-emerge with greater intensity.

This is where prayer and supplication are needed to combat this strategy. Anxiety often thrives when the mind attempts to carry burdens that were never meant to be sustained part from God. Prayer is not merely communication; it is an act of surrender where trust replaces striving and dependence upon God overcomes the torment of anxious thoughts. The peace of God is not produced through human control, but through remaining anchored in the presence, truth, and faithfulness of Christ even when circumstances remain unchanged.

*"Be careful for nothing; but in every thing by prayer and supplication with thanksgiving let your requests be made known unto God." — **Philippians 4:6 KJV***

Spiritually, false peace functions the same way. Sin becomes tolerable until pressure exposes its instability. The Queen's system trains the soul to self-soothe rather than to surrender.

Her prophets declare, "*You are enough.*"
The Holy Spirit declares, *"My grace is sufficient for thee."*

— **2 Corinthians 12:9 KJV** The first reinforces self; God's way transforms it. Jeremiah continues,

"Were they ashamed when they had committed abomination? nay, they were not at all ashamed, neither could they blush: therefore shall they fall among them that fall."
— Jeremiah 8:12 KJV

When conviction is removed, shame eventually disappears; and when shame disappears, sensitivity is lost. The Queen's ministry is to make rebellion appear acceptable. She quiets the conscience through affirmation and minimizes the weight of disobedience by reducing its seriousness.

She whispers, *"It's not that deep."*
But the absence of conviction is not maturity—it is evidence of spiritual decay.

God asks through Jeremiah:

"Is there no balm in Gilead; is there no physician there? why then is not the health of the daughter of my people recovered?"
— Jeremiah 8:22 KJV

The ***balm of Gilead*** was a real healing substance it is an herb resin, yet spiritually it represents truth that penetrates beyond the surface. The question carries divine grief: the remedy exists, yet the people prefer what only imitates healing a *placebo.*

Modern Insight

In today's world, emotional healing is often marketed more than spiritual repentance. We see therapies without truth, mindfulness without submission to the master, and self-love without surrender. This is the Queen's system—presenting wholeness without holiness. It appears gentle, yet it erodes discernment.

She teaches that discomfort must always be avoided, when some discomfort is God directed. The Holy Spirit convicts in order to correct, while the Queen comforts to maintain control. The serpent is not careless in his approach; he is calculated, observant, and precise in how he engages the mind. His strategy is not built on force but on influence, not on chaos but on careful design. This is why Scripture instructs, *"Be ye therefore wise as serpents, and harmless as doves."* — **Matthew 10:16 KJV**

The command is not to imitate the serpent's nature, but to understand his strategy. Wisdom recognizes patterns, discerns motives, and refuses to be unaware of devices, while humility ensures that discernment never becomes pride. The serpent operates through calculation, but the believer must operate through consecration.

To be wise as a serpent is to remain aware of how deception moves—how it studies, how it suggests, how it waits.

But to remain as a dove is to stay pure in intention, gentle in spirit, and submitted in heart. One guards perception, the other guards your posture. One equips the mind; the other protects the soul.

Together, they form the balance required for spiritual authority: awareness without corruption, discernment without pride, and understanding without compromise.

Contrast: The True Comforter

"But the Comforter, which is the Holy Ghost, whom the Father will send in my name, he shall teach you all things, and bring all things to your remembrance, whatsoever I have said unto you."
— John 14:26 KJV

The true Comforter does not flatter he does not remind you to condemn, but to transform you. Where the Queen encourages avoidance of pain, the Spirit leads believers to face it through grace, bringing truth into the light of memory until it no longer governs the response of darkness.

Consequences of Counterfeit Comfort

1. **Emotional Dependency** — *constant need for reassurance replaces stability in Christ*
2. **Delayed Deliverance** — *surface peace postpones true repentance*
3. **Loss of Conviction** — *conscience becomes dull and holiness feels restrictive*
4. **False Movements** — *emotional expression is mistaken for anointing, and crowds are mistaken for confirmation*

God's Way – The Real Healing Process

God heals through His truth, not avoidance and false security and misplaced trust as the Queen would have you to think. When His Word is confronted, it often cuts—but the purpose of the cut is for cleansing, not harm. What is hidden must be brought to light ***Luke 8:17*** and ***John 3:20-21*** this will show you the pattern that what is concealed must be exposed. Her trick is to keep one in bondage to her idols to avoid corrections needed to walk in liberty. Emotional reassurance must cease for Gods truth to be revealed.

"For the word of God is quick, and powerful, and sharper than any twoedged sword."
— Hebrews 4:12 KJV

The Lord's restoration begins when self-soothing ends. This is where peace emerges when what is hidden is brought into light. God does not offer peace apart from this process. Endurance is definitely learned. He establishes peace through transformation. The cutting away and exposure is part of the repentance and refining process. ***Romans 5:3-5***

Revelation Insight

The Lord is raising a people who will not mistake sedation for salvation. He will teach them to prefer his scalpel over their silence. They will find peace in his presence, not in their performance. The counterfeit comforter relieves pain without restoring holiness, while the Holy Spirit heals through holiness. The Queen quiets emotion, Christ restores identity. What she offers brings about numbness; what He gives renews bringing a refreshment to the soul and spirit.

"Thou wilt keep him in perfect peace, whose mind is stayed on thee: because he trusteth in thee."
— Isaiah 26:3 KJV

Peace is not an emotion; it is the result of a mind anchored in truth. Where emotion once governed, revelation now rules and reign.

The Ambition of the Soul: Emotional Manipulation and Power

Definition of Ambition:
Ambition is the drive to achieve distinction without submission. In God, it is refined into purpose; in the flesh, it expresses itself as performance. When ambition is not crucified, it matures into manipulation—the attempt to move divine hands through emotional leverage rather than surrendered obedience. This is one of the Queen of Heaven's most refined strategies: she trains individuals to cloak disobedience in the language of desire, making what originates in self-appear as devotion to God.

"Then came to him the mother of Zebedee's children with her sons, worshipping him, and desiring a certain thing of him.
And he said unto her, what wilt thou? She saith unto him, Grant that these my two sons may sit, the one on thy right hand, and the other on the left, in thy kingdom."
— **Matthew 20:20–21 KJV**

Here, worship becomes negotiation. The posture appears reverent, yet within it is a request shaped by personal aspiration. The mother bows, but her bow conceals expectations. Her request is not open rebellion—it is ambition framed through relationship. She assumes that proximity grants position, that access guarantees elevation. This is the Queen's whisper: "*If it feels deeply enough, it must be aligned with God.*"

Revelation Insight

The spirit of ambition recreates the Garden exchange in a different form. Eve desired wisdom to become *"as gods,"* while the mother of Zebedee sought position to rise *above men.* Both desires were presented in a way that appeared aligned with purpose, yet both bypassed submission. Emotional intensity became the justification for advancement. Jesus immediately dismantles this system:

"Ye know that the princes of the Gentiles exercise dominion over them... But it shall not be so among you: but whosoever will be great among you, let him be your minister."
— **Matthew 20:25–26 KJV**

Christ redefines greatness entirely. Where ambition seeks recognition, He establishes service. Where the Queen teaches that authority confirms affection, Jesus reveals that authority flows from stewardship born of surrender. Ambition reaches for status and acceptance; a true anointing reaches for God's obedience.

Psychological Insight

Human ambition often forms where affirmation was absent or conditional. When love must be earned, identity becomes performance driven. What begins as a desire to be valued becomes a pattern of striving to be validated, one of the serpent's modern-day strategies. This is why discerning the difference is essential for survival.

This produces a form of spirituality centered on visibility rather than transformation, a need to be seen that replaces the call to be sanctified.

Worth becomes tied to recognition instead of obedience. As a result, ministry shifts from altar to platform, and calling becomes confused with exposure.

The System of Manipulation

1. ***Desire*** *— the soul senses neglect or lack of recognition*
2. ***Emotion*** *— the internal pressure for acknowledgment increases*
3. ***Negotiation*** *— prayer shifts from surrender to persuasion*
4. ***Disappointment*** *— unmet expectation gives birth to offense*
5. ***Accusation*** *— the heart begins to question God's fairness*

This pattern reflects the Queen's system: desire leading to control, control leading to frustration, and frustration opening the door to rebellion. The serpent does not need hatred toward God; he needs you to love desire and plant doubt.

"Let nothing be done through strife or vainglory; but in lowliness of mind let each esteem other better than themselves."
— **Philippians 2:3 KJV**

Contrast – God's Way

True promotion comes by alignment with God, a relationship that needs cultivating, not fixated on emotions. He elevates through our obedience, not through opportunities that man say is from God.

The world would tell you otherwise. He entrusts authority to those who value His will above their own recognition.

"Humble yourselves therefore under the mighty hand of God, that he may exalt you in due time."
— **1 Peter 5:6 KJV**

"Due time" dismantles urgency-driven ambition. Where the Queen insists on immediacy, God cultivates patience.

One pressures; the other prepares, waiting on God requires ***faith driven obedience.***

Faith-driven obedience is not built upon emotion, convenience, or visible certainty, but upon confidence in the character, wisdom, and authority of God even when the full outcome has not yet been revealed.

Throughout Scripture, obedience often required movement before understanding, trust before evidence, and surrender before clarity. True faith does not merely agree with God in words; it responds to Him through action, submission, endurance, and reverence for His Word.

Obedience rooted in faith remains steadfast because it is anchored in who God is rather than in changing circumstances or personal comfort.

• *"For we walk by faith, not by sight."* — **2 Corinthians 5:7 KJV**
• Faith responds to God even when every detail is not visible.
• Obedience reveals where trust has truly been placed.
• Delayed obedience often becomes compromise when conviction is ignored.
• God strengthens those who remain willing to follow His direction above personal understanding.
• *"Trust in the LORD with all thine heart; and lean not unto thine own understanding."* — ***Proverbs 3:5 KJV***

Consequences of Emotional Ambition

1. ***Premature Exposure*** — *stepping into visibility before character is formed*
2. ***Prophetic Distortion*** — *speaking from desire instead of discernment*
3. ***Relational Breakdown*** — *comparison replacing community*
4. ***Diminished Sensitivity*** — *the voice of the Spirit becomes secondary to internal impulse*

Modern Insight

This same dynamic fuels spiritual branding, performance-driven ministry, and comparison culture. When worship becomes centered on applause, when prophetic voices pursue platforms, and when success is measured by following rather than faithfulness, the Queen of Heaven has established influence in new forms.

God's Counter-System

God does not remove ambition—He redeems it by directing it toward servanthood. In His Kingdom, elevation is found through humility.

"Let this mind be in you, which was also in Christ Jesus... But made himself of no reputation, and took upon him the form of a servant."
— Philippians 2:5–7 KJV

The mind of Christ dismantles ambition rooted in self by redefining success. Obedience becomes victory, and waiting becomes the assignment when required. Where the Queen says, *prove yourself*, the King says, *remain in Me*.

Revelation Insight

God is exposing ambition that has been mistaken for anointing. He is teaching His servants to discover strength in purity and promotion in patience. Those who reject manipulation will carry out this manifestation.

Ambition without surrender produces control through emotion. Humility, however, produces authority that endures. The Queen manipulates a lot of people through desire; Christ governs through death to self.

"If any man will come after me, let him deny himself, and take up his cross, and follow me."
— Matthew 16:24 KJV

To deny self is to remove the throne from emotion. Each cross carried dismantles another layer of control, and from that surrender emerges authority capable of restoring others.

The Inner Civil War: The Psychology of Rebellion

Definition of Civil War:
A *civil war* is conflict within a single body where both sides claim legitimacy. Spiritually, it is the internal contest between a redeemed spirit and an unrenewed soul. The serpent's preferred battlefield is not the external world, it is the believer's mind, where truth and memory compete for authority.

"For that which I do I allow not: for what I would, that do I not; but what I hate, that do I."
— **Romans 7:15 KJV**

Paul describes a state of inner contradiction—a man aligned with righteousness in desire yet pulled toward disobedience in response. This is not hypocrisy; it is disorder or hierarchy confusion. The spirit recognizes truth, while the soul retains impressions shaped by past experiences or pleasure. When the mind has not been renewed, emotional impulses continue to direct behavior even when intention has been sanctified.

Definition of Rebellion

Rebellion is not limited to resisting God's command; it is sustained loyalty to self-will. It begins as self-preservation and gradually develops into self-exaltation self-deception at its best. The Queen of Heaven system thrives in this environment because it persuades believers that their feelings carry authority.

"For the flesh lusteth against the Spirit, and the Spirit against the flesh: and these are contrary the one to the other: so that ye cannot do the things that ye would."
— ***Galatians 5:17 KJV***

Revelation Insight

Rebellion is reasoning shaped by emotion rather than governed by revelation. The serpent introduces delay disguised as safety, "*You can obey later—secure yourself first.*" Each postponed act of obedience reinforces a pattern of hesitation. Over time, this rhythm becomes familiar, and what once required resistance becomes easier to repeat. When comforts and securities and self- centered lifestyles are challenged most often cynical and skeptical attitudes are presented. This is where justification of inconsistences are, God is calling for His people to change the way life is lived on the inside and not appearing to be righteous on the outside.

Psychological Insight

Cognitive dissonance describes the tension that arises when belief and behavior conflict. The mind seeks to reduce that tension by adjusting one to accommodate the other. Spiritually, when justification replaces repentance, rebellion becomes reinforced through reasoning. Grace is then misapplied not as a means of transformation, but as permission for continuation.

"Ever learning, and never able to come to the knowledge of the truth."

— **2 Timothy 3:7 KJV**

"For the time will come when they will not endure sound doctrine; but after their own lusts shall they heap to themselves teachers, having itching ears." — **2 Timothy 4:3 KJV**

Symptoms of the Inner War

1. ***Emotional Exhaustion*** — *ongoing guilt without measurable growth*
2. ***Inconsistent Focus*** — *cycles of intensity followed by disengagement*

3. ***Selective Obedience** — responsiveness in affirmation, resistance in correction*
4. ***Rationalized Sin** — redefining bondage as process*

"O wretched man that I am! who shall deliver me from the body of this death?
I thank God through Jesus Christ our Lord."
— **Romans 7:24–25 KJV.** Deliverance begins with recognition and gratitude, not condemnation. Paul does not resolve the conflict through denial but through dependence. *"Through Jesus Christ our Lord" marks* a transfer of authority—where the spirit assumes leadership over what once governed the soul.

The Queen's Strategy

She sustains internal conflict through emotional fatigue. She convinces you that struggle is failure, then offers compromise as relief. Her message suggests that difficulty indicates misalignment. Her theology: *"If it feels impossible, it can't be God."* Yet the cross reveals the opposite—what is difficult is often the path through which grace is established.

Consequences of Surrender to Rebellion

– Loss of authority; prayer becomes routine rather than relational
– Distorted perception; sin appears understandable rather than destructive
– Spiritual inconsistency; progress interrupted by self-withdrawal.

God's Way – Integration Through Renewal

"And be renewed in the spirit of your mind."
— **Ephesians 4:23 KJV**

Renewal is the re-education of the soul by the spirit until obedience becomes the natural response. The Spirit of God restructures internal reactions, replacing impulse with discernment.

"Walk in the Spirit, and ye shall not fulfil the lust of the flesh."
— **Galatians 5:16 KJV**

The phrase "shall not" reflects a shift in authority, not an increase in effort. When the Spirit leads, rebellion no longer directs behavior.

Revelation Insight

The LORD is teaching his sons and daughters to govern the inner nation of their spiritual life; your thoughts will no longer oppose his will. Through revelation, he will quiet the internal warfare, and peace will become your rule.

"Peace I leave with you, my peace I give unto you: not as the world giveth, give I unto you. Let not your heart be troubled, neither let it be afraid"

— ***John 14:27 KJV***

Rebellion is psychological bondage presented as independence. When emotion defines truth, the Queen of Heaven governs quietly. When the Spirit renews perception, peace establishes order, and obedience becomes the language of the soul.

"Great peace have they which love thy law: and nothing shall offend them."
— **Psalm 119:165 KJV**

Peace is not the absence of tension—it is the result of proper order. The internal conflict resolves when emotion submits to the authority of the Word.

The Tragedy of Emotional Vows: Worship Without Wisdom

Definition of Emotional Vow:
An *emotional vow* is a promise formed in intensity without revelation. It is devotion driven by urgency rather than direction. It

carries sincerity yet lacks structure. Emotion gives it strength, but truth has not shaped it.

Judges 11:29–31 KJV

Jephthah stands as an example of empowerment without stability. The Spirit came upon him for battle, yet his internal foundation had not been formed for wisdom. His vow was not insincere, it was ungoverned. He spoke beyond instruction, and when victory came, the cost of his words demanded what God never required.

Revelation Insight

Jephthah represents a generation that carries power without maturity. The Queen of Heaven manipulates this condition by encouraging passion without grounding.

She persuades individuals that sacrifice validates obedience, when in truth, obedience defines sacrifice.

"To obey is better than sacrifice..." — **1 Samuel 15:22 KJV**

God's Way — Covenant Over Vow

God does not require vows, he never asked for it; He establishes covenant obedience to his word, man is the one that initiated vows. A vow relies on emotions and covenant relies on revelation.

"My covenant will I not break..." — **Psalm 89:34 KJV**

Covenant provides stability, continuity, and grace. It does not produce loss, it produces transformation.

Revelation Insight

The LORD is breaking the spirit of demonic worship; in the earth He is teaching his people that surrender is not for entertainment. His yoke is easy because His wisdom carries an anointing that will not be imitated. He will deliver His children from the guilt that drives them to make promises He never requested. Jephthah's vow warns us that passion without the right perception destroys what obedience would have maintained. Emotional vows produce burnt offerings God never commanded. The queen of heaven celebrates burnout; the LORD of Heaven and Earth call for wisdom.

"Wisdom is the principal thing; therefore get wisdom: and with all thy getting get understanding."
— **Proverbs 4:7 KJV**

Wisdom sanctifies your worship. It ensures that what begins with zeal ends in fruit producing attributes, not rotten fruit that has to be cut off. Which leads to a fruitless life resulting in spiritual death. True surrender is not an emotional display, it is spiritual alignment.

"Come unto me, all ye that labour and are heavy laden, and I will give you rest."
— **Matthew 11:28 KJV**

God doesn't need your vow to bless you; He needs your trust to transform you.

Witchcraft, Soothsayers, Moon & Star Worship Definition of Witchcraft

Witchcraft is the spiritual practice of influencing outcomes through unauthorized power, where control replaces submission and desire seeks to override divine order. It is control dressed as revelation and manipulation presented as discernment. In Scripture, witchcraft is never limited to ritual or external expression, it is rebellion carried out with evil intention, a deliberate attempt to secure results for the benefit of oneself apart from obedience. Your motives and intentions matter to the Lord it determines what spirit is truly operating inwardly. We must always bible check ourselves.

"For rebellion is as the sin of witchcraft, and stubbornness is as iniquity and idolatry."
— 1 Samuel 15:23 KJV

Witchcraft begins where submission ends. When people stop trusting God's process, they start seeking control through a power that unknowing is a demonic power that is designed to deceive. The Queen of Heaven teaches witchcraft through emotion that leads to ritualistic acts. She persuades the soul that waiting is unnecessary and that outcomes can be accelerated through desire. Her whisper is cunning but strategic, *"You don't have to wait—you can manifest it."* In this way, dependence is replaced with self-direction, and self-direction is mislabeled as faith. Many operate in evil practices in ignorance; this is the serpent's strategy to win soul for his kingdom.

Definition of Soothsayer

A *soothsayer* is one who receives hidden knowledge through divination, sorcery and magic rather than true knowledge from God, someone who speaks about the future without alignment to the Spirit of Truth. The root word *"sooth"* implies comfort, this insight may sound true, but its foundation rooted in evil practices.

Soothsaying is forbidden knowledge for comfort appealing to your emotions, your flesh and not for edification that leads to correction true insight given through the Holy Spirit. It's what happens when emotions demand foresight before obedience has matured.

This is originated from the kingdom of darkness. It offers answers without alignment and direction without transformation bring life.

"There shall not be found among you... a consulter with familiar spirits, or a wizard, or a necromancer. For all that do these things are an abomination unto the LORD."
— **Deuteronomy 18:10–12 KJV**

The queen's system flourishes wherever people prioritize their outcome over their relationship with God. It promises insight without repentance and knowledge without intimacy. We are to worship the Lord in Spirit and in truth. It offers a form clarity while bypassing surrender to the will of God. The Lord is sovereign and will not be mocked. As believers we must be intentional in what and who we will submit to. Ignorance is one of the serpent's greatest weapons. These were the type of practices passed down as traditions and some today still have the delusion that it is ok to participate in evil. She imitates divine timing by synchronizing human reactions with cycles, seasons, sensations, and internal shifts until individuals begin to follow those false impressions instead of God's instruction.

Definition of Moon & Star Worship

This ancient form of idolatry established authority through cycles rather than covenant. The moon governed emotion and fertility, while the stars were interpreted as indicators of destiny, and the queen of heaven positioned herself as ruler over these patterns, creating a system where timing became a tool of control. What was meant to be governed by God's order was redirected into systems that shaped behavior through disobedience rather than obedience.

Over time, people began to look for cycles for direction, allowing external patterns to influence internal decisions.

This shifted reliance away from God's Word and placed it into created signs that were never meant to lead.

In this way, authority was cunningly transferred, quietly through what people chose to follow.

"There shall not be found among you any one that maketh his son or his daughter to pass through the fire, or that useth divination, or an observer of times, or an enchanter, or a witch,
Or a charmer, or a consulter with familiar spirits, or a wizard, or a necromancer.
For all that do these things are an abomination unto the LORD."
— **Isaiah 47:12–13 KJV**

Isaiah reveals Babylon—the center of this system the queen's throne—as *wearied sorceries.* This exhaustion comes from attempting to control outcomes that were never meant to be managed outside of obedience. They labored to predict and preserve what could only be secured through surrender. This is fatigue of self-managed destiny. Only revelation that is given through total surrender and obedience to the Holy Spirit gives divine insight.

Revelation Insight

The queen's system teaches what can be called *emotional astrology* a pattern where internal states are treated as indicators of timing. She persuades individuals that their feelings follow cosmic timing instead of covenant truth. This is why moods shift with seasons and spiritual warfare spikes at certain times of the year. This is why prayer must become a priority to combat the strategy against the kingdom of darkness. You must hinger and thirst for righteousness.

The serpent studies these emotional calendars, most times people move according to routine rather than revelation. When the behavioral model patterns become consistent, they can be predicted.

Psychological Insight

In behavioral science, ***circadian rhythms*** regulate physical energy cycles. In the soul, emotional rhythms can begin to shape decision-making. When individuals begin to respond according to their emotions rather than spiritual direction, patterns form this is when you are in your carnal state not living according to the spirit.

Over time, these patterns create expectancy. The enemy does not need new strategies when responses follow established rhythms. He simply waits for the moment when the cycle repeats an optune time.

God's Way — True Divine Timing

"To everything there is a season, and a time to every purpose under the heaven."
— **Ecclesiastes 3:1 KJV**

God's timing is covenantal, not cyclical in the sense of control. Seasons are not given to manipulate the behavior but to mature character. Delay is not nonexistent, it is development. Where the Queen pressures for immediate action, God cultivates endurance and alignment to bring forth His perfect will.

Where the Holy Spirit says wait, the serpent's system introduces urgency. Where the Word says trust, the serpent's system encourages control. True timing is not discovered through emotional shifts but through obedience. We are to be led by the Holy Spirit. This is a principle key factor to life survival to govern your life in this world today.

Modern Insight

- Manifestation practices that replace prayer with declaration
- Horoscopes presented as personality insight "energy"
- Believers checking internal states or "vibes" before consulting Scripture
- Ministries promoting timing without grounding in truth

These are modern altars of expression of astrology the queen uses. They appear insightful, yet they are a part of an evil kingdom. They generate movement without formation and activity without discernment. This is simply deception founded on ignorance.

"For false Christs and false prophets shall rise, and shall shew signs and wonders, to seduce, if it were possible, even the elect."
— **Mark 13:22 KJV**

The Queen uses signs not to reveal Christ, but to redirect attention away from Him. She creates dependence on experiences, cycles, the next spiritual event—keeping individuals waiting for the next emotional high rather than remaining rooted in God's presence.

In doing so, she replaces the relationship with God as a strategy of deception, and communion as demonic cycles. This is a kingdom of darkness strategy cycle.

Revelation Insight

The LORD is severing his people from emotional calendars.
He is destroying the witchcraft of rebellion that comes from self-managed destiny. His Spirit will teach you divine stillness again.
You will discern by the covenant of the word and the help of the Holy Spirit, not by climate of the world.

Consequences of the Queen's Timing System:

1. **Perpetual Delay** – waiting for perfect emotional conditions before obeying.
2. **Prophetic Confusion** – misinterpreting warfare as issues of timing.
3. **Weariness** – recurring cycles of hope and despair that weaken faith.
4. **Idolatry of Atmosphere** – serving the feeling sensation of God rather than God Himself.

The Mind of Christ - True Authority Over Time:

"It is not for you to know the times or the seasons, which the Father hath put in his own power."
— **Acts 1:7 KJV**

Jesus dismantled astrological anxiety with this statement.

Timing belongs to God; obedience belongs to us.

Faith waits with intention, not anxiously awaiting but to *be anxious for nothing, but through prayer and supplication with thanksgiving.* ***Philippians 4:6*** the Lord instructions are intentional for victory.

The Holy Spirit releases the mind from the bondage of speculation, a form of captivity that restricts growth and prevents spiritual fruit from maturing in one's life.

Revelation Insight

The Queen of Heaven weaponizes time to govern the emotion; Christ redeems the time to establish His purpose.

Do you see the pattern yet…?

One binds through prediction; the other liberates through presence. her worshippers pursue cycles, His sons steward the they are in seasons.

"Redeeming the time, because the days are evil."
— **Ephesians 5:16 KJV**

To redeem time is to rescue moments from manipulation. When the Holy Spirit leads, delay becomes discipline, and waiting becomes a time of worship.

Familiar Spirits & Emotional Nostalgia –The Queen's Memory Network

What is a **Familiar Spirit** A familiar spirit is a demonic intelligence that mimics relationships and old cycles. The word "familiar" comes from the Latin *familiaris*, meaning "household."

It describes a spirit that appears at ease because it has learned your patterns, your preferences, and your pain.

Its function is to maintain emotional control — ensuring that even when the circumstances shift, your responses remain consistent.

"Regard not them that have familiar spirits, neither seek after wizards, to be defiled by them: I am the LORD your God."
— **Leviticus 19:31 KJV**

Familiar spirits operate as emotional archivists.
They gather data from your history about what angers you, what soothes you, what tempts you, what affirms you and they reintroduce those conditions when you approach deliverance.

They are the unseen enforcers of the Queen of Heaven's infrastructure.

Definition of Nostalgia

Nostalgia is the longing for a moment that no longer exists.

Spiritually, it becomes emotional idolatry, the elevation of memory above movement. The queen uses nostalgia to turn yesterday into a sanctuary and the past into a prison, snares and bondages.
She keeps individuals revisiting former emotions under the appearance of reflection.

"Should not a people seek unto their God? for the living to the dead?"
— **Isaiah 8:19 KJV**

Isaiah exposes the contradiction seeking direction from what has already expired. To *"seek unto the dead"* is to depend on what no longer carries life, look at it this way, when memory becomes a mentor, stagnation becomes the result and progression is impossible.

Revelation Insight

Familiar spirits attach themselves to emotional memories that were never surrendered to God. They speak through recollection, shaping your interpretation until the pain begins to influence your perception.

They make bondage appear like belonging because it is recognizable.

This is why many return to relationships, environments, or habits they once prayed to escape the emotion that resembles home, a safe space.

Psychological Insight

Neuroscience identifies engrams — the brain's imprints of significant experiences. When revisited, these engrams reactivate the same internal chemistry connected to the original event. Spiritually, familiar spirits exploit this replay. They trigger memory to reintroduce former conditions. Deliverance, therefore, requires not only removal but renewal of interpretation.

"For the weapons of our warfare are not carnal, but mighty through God to the pulling down of strong holds;Casting down imaginations, and every high thing that exalteth itself against the knowledge of God, and bringing into captivity every thought to the obedience of Christ."

— 2 Corinthians 10:4–5 KJV

Definition of Stronghold

A *stronghold* is a memory fortified by emotion and justified by reasoning. It becomes a familiar space within the soul where false conclusions remain unchallenged. The queen of heaven uses strongholds as altars of remembrance, emotional territories where past pain continues to influence present response.

Speculation — Infusive
Speculation is the mental habit of attempting to interpret outcomes, motives, or timing without revelation from God. It is the mind reaching beyond its authority to construct meaning where obedience has not yet been established. Rooted in uncertainty, it produces internal narratives that feel insightful but are disconnected from truth. Spiritually, speculation is a subtle form of control—it replaces trust with assumption, patience with prediction, and faith with self-generated understanding. It keeps the soul in motion but prevents the spirit from leading, creating a cycle where thought replaces discernment and imagination overrides instruction. Left unchecked, speculation becomes a form of bondage, because it trains the mind to respond to possibilities instead of promises, ultimately stunting spiritual growth and delaying the fruit that only obedience can produce.

Consequences of the Queen's Memory Network

1. **Cycle Reinforcement** – repeated failures at consistent emotional intervals.
2. **Selective Amnesia** – remembering pleasure while dismissing the pain.
3. **Emotional Paralyzation** – inability to embrace new seasons because former ones remain honored.
4. **False Discernment** – interpreting new opportunities through the language of unresolved wounds.

Modern Insight

– Revisiting past relationships for closure.
– Listening to songs that reactivate emotional seasons.
– Associating conviction with past rejection.
– Romanticizing past sin as "simpler times."

The queen system thrives where nostalgia replaces gratitude. Gratitude thanks God for what He has done. Nostalgia grieves what He has removed. Gratitude matures, while nostalgia preserves the attachment. What begins as remembrance can quietly become a longing for, when left unchecked it can begin to pull the heart backward instead of allowing it to move forward. Instead of recognizing God's hand in progression, nostalgia keeps attention fixed on what is no longer meant to remain. Over time, this shifts trust, causing a person to measure the present against the past rather than receiving what God is doing now. In a new way, attachment is maintained, not through open rebellion, but through a quiet resistance to release what God has already moved beyond.

God's Way – The Sanctification of Memory

"Brethren... forgetting those things which are behind..."
— **Philippians 3:13 KJV**

Paul is not describing removal, but release from influence. To forget is to withdraw emotional permission from the past.

The Holy Spirit sanctifies your memory by redefining its function your story becomes a testimony, not torment which is a device of the enemy to keep you in bondage.

Prophetic Insight

The LORD is reclaiming the memory gates of his people.
The past will no longer prophesy your future He knows the plans He has for you. The places where deception, built altars will become the sites of His presence. He is removing nostalgia and replacing it with His supernatural vision downloaded from His Spirit. That will bring forth an everlasting inheritance.

The Queen's Counterfeit

You must remember the queen is a deceiver and manipulator. She invites people to *"remember when,"* but never allows them to *"behold now.* "She turns healing into heritage, keeping individuals loyal to what wounded them. This is ***emotional witchcraft*** — preservation of pain disguised as reflection and honor.

Self-Check Strategy –

1. Identify the emotional memories that trigger old reactions.
2. Repent for idolizing past versions of yourself.
3. Invite the Holy Spirit to reinterpret your past through truth.
4. Replace nostalgia with gratitude, pain with purpose.

"He restoreth my soul: he leadeth me in the paths of righteousness for his name's sake."

— **Psalm 23:3 KJV**

To restore is to return to original intention. When the Lord restores the soul, He rewires your memory to glorify Him. What once replayed the trauma now testifies of triumph victory is yours.

The familiar spirit loses access because the emotional address has changed know that the devil will try and wait for another chance to try you. We must fight the good fight of faith daily to survive.

"Fight the good fight of faith, lay hold on eternal life, whereunto thou art also called, and hast professed a good profession before many witnesses."
— 1 Timothy 6:12 KJV

Revelation Insight

Familiar spirits thrive in emotional nostalgia; the Spirit of Truth operates through renewed perspective. The Queen of Heaven binds through recollection you must be able to discern the difference; Christ frees us through revelation. Deliverance does not require forgetting your story — it requires rewriting its meaning.

"*Old things are passed away, behold all things have become new..."*

— **2 Corinthians 5:17 KJV**

When your mind aligns with this truth, yesterday loses jurisdiction. As a believer you become unpredictable again. And where predictability ends, the serpent's strategy collapses.

The Mind of Christ: Heaven's Counter-System

Definition of the Mind of Christ

The ***Mind of Christ*** is the divine consciousness that interprets reality through obedience, not emotion. It is perception sanctified by presence — seeing as God sees, thinking as His Word thinks, and choosing as His Spirit leads. You must be born again of the Holy Spirit to receive this revelation. Where the Queen of Heaven builds her throne in the limbic system, (the seat of emotion) Christ establishes His kingdom in renewed thought as you take on a new citizenship status in his government.

"Let this mind be in you, which was also in Christ Jesus:
Who, being in the form of God, thought it not robbery to be equal with God, But made himself of no reputation, and took upon him the form of a servant."
— **Philippians 2:5–7 KJV**

"Jesus answered and said unto him, Verily, verily, I say unto thee, Except a man be born again, he cannot see the kingdom of God."
— John 3:3 KJV

"Jesus answered, Verily, verily, I say unto thee, Except a man be born of water and of the Spirit, he cannot enter into the kingdom of God."
— John 3:5 KJV

The Queen's system thrives wherever emotion is enthroned above truth. She does not begin by demanding open rebellions, she cultivates misalignment. She trains the soul to trust in self-reliance above divine instruction until discernment weakens and conviction feels intrusive it confronts what most rather ignore. Over time, what once required justification becomes instinct. This is how deception matures—quietly, progressively, systemically.

But the LORD never leaves corruption unchallenged. Where seduction builds through repetition, He restores through revelation. The answer to emotional governance is not suppression—it is replacement. The Queen's system must be dethroned, not managed. And that dethroning begins in the mind.

We must remember that the *LORD psychology* is **humility.** In the Queen's system it is pride, emotion seeks elevation; in Christ's system, revelation requires surrender. The mind of Christ is not weak—it is strength governed by yielding to his direction. It does not contend with pain; it assigns purpose to it.

It does not react to pressure; it interprets it through obedience.

Revelation Insight

The mind of Christ dismantles emotional idolatry by redefining your value. Where the Queen teaches that power proves your identity, Christ reveals that obedience uncovers it. He did not cling to status. He embraced service. Every miracle He performed flowed from alignment, not assertion, from communion rather than compulsion. His authority was not driven by impulse but governed by divine order. He has given every born-again believer the power to tread on the head of the serpent.

"Behold, I give unto you power to tread on serpents and scorpions, and over all the power of the enemy: and nothing shall by any means hurt you."
— Luke 10:19 KJV

"Though he were a Son, yet learned he obedience by the things which he suffered;"

— Hebrews 5:8 KJV

This is why Scripture declares, *"For God hath not given us the spirit of fear; but of power, and of love, and of a sound mind."* **(2 Timothy 1:7 KJV).** A *sound mind* is a restored way of perceiving clarity. It is not the absence of emotion, but the proper ordering of it. Fear no longer dictates direction, and anxiety no longer advises decisions. Power and love now to function in harmony because order has been reestablished within. The LORD has given the power to rule and reign in the earth through his Spirit.

Definition of Sound Mind

To be *sound* is to be whole—complete and internally governed by truth. A sound mind does not contradict its confession; it submits to the Word and responds accordingly. It does not fluctuate with circumstance but remains anchored in revelation. This is God's model of wholeness—truth established first, experience following. For *"God is not the author of confusion, but of peace"*

(1 Corinthians 14:33 KJV), and where His order is present, clarity becomes the natural result.

The Queen's counterfeit offers self-awareness without sanctification. She promotes introspection that centers the self rather than crucifies it. She uses knowledge of wounds to justify rebellion instead of directing it toward redemption. Her message is crafty and cunning, "Heal yourself to find peace." But Christ speaks differently, "Find Me and receive peace."

"And be not conformed to this world: but be ye transformed by the renewing of your mind that ye may prove what is that good, and acceptable, and perfect, will of God."
*—**Romans 12:2 KJV**.*

When you decide to give up your life and follow Christ you give up your ideologies, the world's way and surrender to living life God's way. Transformation begins where conformity is rejected. The Greek word for transformed—*metamorphoō*—is the same word used for Christ's transfiguration. This reveals that renewal does not merely adjust your behavior; it unveils your divine nature. A renewed mind becomes a living reflection of Christ Himself, proving the will of God through life, not ritual. The way the Kingdom of God works culture, heredity living life apart from your carnal mind, but through the divine rebirth of His Spirit that bring forth life and peace.

Psychological Insight

Cognitive restructuring in psychology mirrors spiritual renewal, altering thought patterns to influence behavior. But while therapy modifies thoughts, the Holy Spirit uproots them. He crucifies lies at its root. This is not self-improvement; it is identity realignment through truth. As Scripture declares, *"Casting down imaginations... and bringing into captivity every thought to the obedience of Christ;"*

—2 Corinthians 10:5 KJV As affection is repositioned, allegiance follows,

"Set your affection on things above, not on things on the earth. For ye are dead, and your life is hid with Christ in God."

—Colossians 3:2–3 KJV

Where the Queen demands emotional devotion, Christ calls for intellectual surrender. He does not negotiate with the mind—He reigns over it. He commands thoughts to kneel so truth can be revealed. This is a heart posture change that gives birth to a regenerated heart transformation.

The Mind of Christ Produces:

1. **Discernment** – Recognizing God's will beyond feeling lead by the Holy Spirit revealing truth.
2. **Stability** – Consistency in chaos peace within.
3. **Authority** – Dominion over deception walking in kingship.
4. **Clarity** – Seeing temptation as predictable strategy, not mystery not false realities truth that bring light to darkness.

God's System of Thought

The Spirit of God replaces a believer's reaction with revelation. He teaches the believer to pause between impulse and action the holy interval where wisdom intervenes. This is what Jesus modeled when tempted by the devil in the wilderness. A conscious decision must be made between the Spirit and the flesh.

"And when the tempter came to him, he said, If thou be the Son of God, command that these stones be made bread.
But he answered and said, It is written, Man shall not live by bread alone, but by every word that proceedeth out of the mouth of God."
— **Matthew 4:3–4 KJV**

Jesus countered emotional hunger with scriptural order. He didn't deny the feeling; He denied its government. This is why you must study to show yourself approved rightly dividing the word of truth a workman need not to be ashamed of the gospel.

This is how the mind of Christ wins battles, not by avoiding the emotion felt, but by enthroning truth to override the serpent's strategy.

Revelation Insight

He is renewing the mind of His Church so they will no longer process truth through trauma. He is reintroducing discernment where distraction has reigned.

Your reasoning shall be sanctified until logic and love for Christ speak the same language.

Consequences of Rejecting the Renewed Mind:

– Spiritual burnout through emotional decision-making the carnal mind.

– Misinterpreting warfare as rejection.
– Perpetual instability, mistaking a lie for your calling, carnal perception founded on the world's way of thinking.

The Result of Receiving the Renewed Mind:
– Prophetic perception grounded in Scripture.
– Emotional equilibrium during trials. Peace founded in truth of God's word.
– Capacity to love enemies without losing boundaries.
– Clarity of assignment without addiction to affirmation.

"Thou wilt keep him in perfect peace, whose mind is stayed on thee: because he trusteth in thee."
— **Isaiah 26:3 KJV**

Peace follows when you focus on truth. The Queen scatters attention through stimulation; Christ gathers focus through stillness.

When the mind is stayed on Him, emotional warfare loses jurisdiction. You must remember her throne sits in feelings; God's throne sits in faith. To receive the mind of Christ you must dethrone the queen permanently. It is the victory of revelation over your reaction, and humility over hysteria, and discipline over desire.

You must choose...

"And ye shall know the truth, and the truth shall make you free."
— **John 8:32 KJV**

The mind of Christ is freedom's architecture. Once this system is installed, the serpent's psychology is destroyed....

Dethroning the Queen

The War in the Heavens and the Renewal of the Mind

Every revelation demands a response. Every truth requires testimony. Exposure without execution leaves systems intact. This is where revelation becomes Spiritual warfare.

The Queen of Heaven system—rooted in emotion, nostalgia, witchcraft, and rebellion—must be **legally and spiritually dethroned.** As a believer you must not only renounce her influence but *nullify* every demonic contract, memory pattern, and emotional altar connected to her network.

This section is a **prophetic litigation** prayer that functions both as a decree and dismantling of agreement. It is not a recitation—it is participation in divine justice giving from the King above all kings. We are to rule and reign remember your stance.

"And hast made us unto our God kings and priests: and we shall reign on the earth."
— Revelation 5:10 KJV

Prayer of Renunciation and Nullification

Heavenly Father,
In the mighty name of **Jesus Christ**, the Son of the Living God,
I step into the courts of heaven under the covenant of the blood of Jesus. By faith in Your Word, I receive the authority of Luke 10:19

"Behold, I give unto you power to tread on serpents and scorpions, and over all the power of the enemy: and nothing shall by any means hurt you."
— Luke 10:19 KJV

Through that power, I now **renounce every allegiance**, conscious or unconscious, that I or my bloodline has ever made with the Queen of Heaven, her familiar spirits, her prophets, or her emotional systems and the power of kingdom of darkness. I repent for every emotional vow, every witchcraft agreement, and every generational practice of it that elevated comfort above covenant and feeling above faith. I withdraw emotional consent from every altar of rebellion, idolatry, or nostalgia. I command every demonic covenant made through ignorance, fear, or trauma to be *nullified by the blood of Jesus Christ.*

In the name of Jesus, I declare:
– Every emotional pattern sustained by familiar spirits is destroyed at the root.
– Every memory that holds pain as prophecy is rewritten by the Spirit of Truth of your word.
– Every whisper from the past that contradicts my purpose is silenced.
– Every counterfeit comfort that numbed conviction is revoked.

In Jesus name, Amen

Prayer for the Renewal of the Mind

Lord Jesus, You are my peace.You are the author and finisher of my faith. Today I submit my thoughts, emotions, and affections to Your lordship. *"Casting down imaginations, and every high thing that exalteth itself against the knowledge of God."*
— 2 Corinthians 10:5 KJV

By Your Spirit, I cast down every imagination that exalts carnal logic above your divine revelation. Let my mind be renewed until I love truth more than a lie, holiness more than deception, and obedience more than outcome. I break every neurological pathway that leads back to sin. I command my emotions to submit to Your truth.

Where my mind has been a battlefield, make it a sanctuary of peace. Where my emotions have been a storm, make them streams of worship. I decree that my feelings are no longer altars for the enemy—they are instruments of praise for my God.

Nullification Decrees: Canceling Demonic Patterns and Assignments

By the blood of Jesus Christ, I decree the **nullification** of every demonic operation, in my life and lineage, known or unknown.

1. **I nullify** every demonic decree released against my destiny through manipulation, witchcraft, or word curses.
2. **I nullify** every emotional loop designed to replay pain, trauma, or shame.
3. **I nullify** every familiar spirit posing as comfort, guidance, or divine memory.
4. **I nullify** every contract of fear that grants access to torment.
5. **I nullify** every generational curse of idolatry, rebellion, and emotional instability.
6. **I nullify** every false prophetic word spoken over my life or unclean altars.
7. **I nullify** every counterfeit dream, vision, and revelation that did not come from the Spirit of Truth.
8. **I nullify** every delay assigned by demonic timing systems or witchcraft calendars.
9. **I nullify** every soul tie formed through emotional dependency or unholy alliances.
10. **I nullify** every system of guilt and performance that makes me feel unworthy of grace.

By the blood of the Lamb, every demonic verdict is reversed, every curse is destroyed, every covenant is canceled null and void.

In Jesus name…Amen

Prophetic Decree of Establishment

Now, in the authority of Christ Jesus,
I decree the establishment of your government within me.

– My emotions are submitted to the Spirit of God.
– My thoughts are sanctified by the Word of God.
– My will is aligned with the purposes of God.
– My memory is healed by the mercy of God.
– My future is secured by the promises of God.

I decree that the Queen of Heaven's throne has been **dethroned** in my life, my family, and my atmosphere.
Her altars are shattered or destroyed.
Her priests are silenced and powerless.
Her rituals are rendered powerless.
Her familiar spirits are cast out and burn by the fire of GOD.
Her timing systems are dismantled and destroyed
Her influence is forbidden from returning.

I enthrone **Jesus Christ** as Lord over my heart, my home, my habits, and my heritage and every generation after me.

He alone rules the rhythm of my emotions and the direction of my days.

"The LORD shall fight for you, and ye shall hold your peace."
— **Exodus 14:14 KJV**

Therefore, I hold my peace as He establishes my victory.

In Jesus name…. Amen

Prophetic Closing Declarations

I decree and declare:

- Every demonic assignment sent to monitor me is blinded by the light of Christ.
- Every trap of manipulation set against my obedience is destroyed.
- Every counterfeit revelation meant to seduce my focus is silenced.
- Every curse of premature death, distraction, or delay is reversed.
- Every emotional wound is healed by the anointing of the oil of joy and the blood of Jesus.
- Every altar of idolatry erected through fear or flattery is consumed by the fire of God.
- Every system of control that attempts to predict my behavior is dismantled and destroyed.
- Every demon of witchcraft and false comfort is evicted now in the name of Jesus Christ.

I decree:

My mind is renewed.
My emotions are sanctified.
My discernment is sharpened.
My vision is restored.
My voice is purified.
My house is under divine order of your word.
My destiny is advancing by divine momentum of your Kingdom.

I decree that I walk in the rhythm of righteousness, the cadence of clarity, and the peace that surpasses understanding.

The Queen's system is overthrown, and your Kingdom's system is enthroned.

"For the kingdom of God is not in word, but in power."
— **1 Corinthians 4:20 KJV**

And I decree that this power now governs my inner world —
in my spirit, in my soul, in my body, and in every sphere of my influence.

In Jesus' mighty name.
Amen.

Finale Chapter Insight

The Queen of Heaven system was an emotional government without Divine permission.
Christ's Kingdom is redemption through Divine order.
When truth rules the soul, every throne built on deception is destroyed.
The serpent loses his prediction. As a believer you walk in Divine power governed only by the mind of Christ.

"The Lord is my light and my salvation; whom shall I fear?
The Lord is the strength of my life; of whom shall I be afraid?"
— **Psalm 27:1 KJV**

You are free…
You are covered…
You are renewed…
You are untouchable in Christ…

— ***You are more than a Conqueror through Christ Jesus …***

Now Rule and Reign….

CHAPTER EIGHT

Balaam's Counsel: When the Enemy Turns from Curse to Corruption

The Blessing That Could Not Be Reversed

Numbers 22–24

When Israel approached the plains of Moab, the surrounding nations did not merely see travelers; they saw a people advancing under covenant promise. Balak, king of Moab, watched Israel's victories with growing alarm. Their survival in the wilderness and their triumphs over opposing kingdoms suggested that ordinary warfare would not succeed against them. What he witnessed was not just military momentum, it was spiritual protection functioning through covenant.

This is the first strategic principle:

Covenant alignment creates a boundary that external opposition cannot penetrate.

Balak therefore turned to what he believed was a spiritual solution. He summoned Balaam, a man known for a prophetic and divinatory power, hoping that a curse spoken over Israel would weaken them before battle.

The encounter between Balaam and the Lord revealed a governing law in spiritual warfare:

"Thou shalt not go with them; thou shalt not curse the people: for they are blessed."
— Numbers 22:12 KJV

The issue was not Balaam's willingness but God's declaration. Israel existed under a covenant blessing given to Abraham and reaffirmed through generations. Because God had already spoken, Balaam could not overturn that word through ritual or pronouncement.

This reveals a second principle:

No outside word can override what God has for your life to be established...

Each attempt to curse Israel resulted instead in a prophetic blessing. The system Balaam operated in was divination, ritual, spoken decree it had no authority over a people secured by God's covenant alignment.

The oracles recorded in Numbers 23–24 make this clear. Balaam himself declared:

"God is not a man, that he should lie… hath he said, and shall he not do it?"
— ***Numbers 23:19 KJV***

The implication was unmistakable. A covenant people aligned with God cannot be dismantled by external curses. Opposition may arise, but divine blessing establishes limits that the enemy cannot cross. But this is where the serpent's strategy shifts. Balaam's repeated failure exposed something critical to the enemy:

If access is denied externally, it must be created internally.

If Israel could not be cursed from the outside, another path had to be found. That path would involve corruption rather than confrontation.

Balaam's Counsel: A Strategy Hidden from Public View

Numbers 31:16; Revelation 2:14

Although Balaam could not pronounce a curse, later Scripture reveals that he did not abandon the effort to weaken Israel. Instead, he changed methods.

When the pronouncement failed, he introduced **environmental strategy**.

The book of Numbers later records the consequence of this counsel:

"Behold, these caused the children of Israel, through the counsel of Balaam, to commit trespass against the LORD in the matter of Peor."
— ***Numbers 31:16 KJV***

The same strategy is mentioned centuries later by Jesus when He addressed the church in Pergamos:

"But I have a few things against thee, because thou hast there them that hold the doctrine of Balaam, who taught Balak to cast a stumbling block before the children of Israel."
— ***Revelation 2:14 KJV***

Notice the language: **"cast a stumbling block."** Balaam did not attack Israel—he **repositioned them**.

"*Cast up… take up the stumbling block out of the way of my people."*
— ***Isaiah 57:14KJV***

"I will go before thee and make the crooked places straight: I will break in pieces the gates of brass, and cut in sunder the bars of iron."
— ***Isaiah 45:2 KJV***

This reveals the core of the strategy:

The enemy does not always need to curse you—he only needs to place you in an environment that contradicts your covenant.

Balaam's insight was strategic. If Israel could be persuaded to compromise their covenant allegiance, the blessing that protected them would weaken from within. Instead of attacking Israel's strength directly, Balaam proposed that Moab draw them into environments where loyalty to the Lord would gradually erode.

This is not immediate rebellion—it is **gradual misalignment**.

This reveals another principle:

Spiritual defeat often begins with relational and environmental exposure, not direct disobedience.

The serpent's strategy frequently operates this way. When hostility fails, seduction becomes the preferred method. When force cannot penetrate, influence begins to reshape.

A covenant people cannot easily be destroyed by force, but they can be persuaded to participate in patterns that undermine their own alignment with God.

This is the doctrine of Balaam:

- **Do not fight them—reposition them.**
- **Do not curse them—entangle them.**
- **Do not oppose them, normalize what weakens them.**

Corruption succeeds where confrontation fails.

Baal-Peor: The Religious System Behind the Seduction

Numbers 25

The counsel Balaam gave to Balak involved more than temptation—it involved a system. Baal-Peor was not a casual idol but a structured environment combining ritual celebration, communal feasting, and sensual worship.

"And Israel abode in Shittim, and the people began to commit whoredom with the daughters of Moab."
— Numbers 25:1 KJV

The process was gradual. Invitation preceded participation.

Moabite women drew the Israelites into sacrificial feasts. That interaction led to shared meals. Those meals were tied to sacrificial rituals. By the time Israel bowed before Baal-Peor, the boundary had already been crossed long before the visible act of idolatry.

In the ancient world, eating food offered to a deity was not neutral—it was an agreement. It signified fellowship with that system.What began as social contact became spiritual compromise.

Baal-Peor: The System Behind the Seduction

Baal-Peor was not merely an idol—it was a system designed to merge worship, pleasure, and identity into one environment.

The name *Baal* means "lord" or "master," while *Peor* is associated with an opening or exposure. Historically and spiritually, Baal-Peor represented a form of worship that removed boundaries—moral, spiritual, and physical. It was not structured around reverence, but around indulgence disguised as devotion. *"They joined themselves also unto Baal peor and ate the sacrifices of the dead."*
— Psalm 106:28 KJV

This system functioned through three integrated layers:

---

1. Sensual Worship (Pleasure as Devotion)
Baal-Peor worship involved sexual immorality as part of ritual practices. What God defined as covenant intimacy was redefined as religious expression. Desire was not resisted but sanctified, normalizing what God forbade. What was meant to be sacred became public and celebrated. God's restrictions were designed to protect intimacy and holiness, but Baal-Peor's rituals redefined, indulgence as worship, turning sinful behavior into religious duties.

What God called a boundary Baal-Peor called a pathway to divine favor twisted as spirituality.

The conscience was conditioned, where conviction was supposed to override this acceptance. This is critical to understand:

The system did not present sin as rebellion—it presented it as worship.

---

2. Communal Feasting (Participation as Agreement)
The Israelites were invited to eat sacrifices connected to the idol. In Scripture, eating is not passive, it is participation.

"And they called the people unto the sacrifices of their gods: and the people did eat and bowed down to their gods."
— ***Numbers 25:2 KJV***

The progression is precise:

- Invitation
- Participation
- Submission

By the time they bowed, they had already agreed.

- **3. Relational Integration (Attachment Before Allegiance)**
  The entry point into Baal-Peor was not theology—it was relationship.

"The people began to commit whoredom with the daughters of Moab."
— ***Numbers 25:1 KJV***

This reveals the strategy:

Attachment was established before allegiance was required.

Once emotional and relational bonds formed, spiritual compromise followed naturally. When relationships form outside of the will of God it affects what and who you believe.

Emotional bonds are built then allegiance is established.

This is called **emotional entanglement.**

From Worship to Economic Allegiance

The system surrounding Baal-Peor extended beyond worship. Like many ancient temple systems, it functioned as a social and economic center. Festivals and sacrificial feasts drew merchants, travelers, and neighboring communities. Participation in rituals often meant participation in trade. This system created an environment where worship and wealth became inseparable. This is often time when people want to justify their actions for allowing compromise to anchor them in to participate in what is not of the Lord.

This created a progression that bound individuals to the system.

1. **Emotional Attraction**
   Celebration lowered resistance. Music, food, and sensuality created engagement that weakened discernment.
2. **Ritual Participation**
   Shared meals connected individuals to the spiritual practices behind them.
3. **Social Integration**
   Relationships formed within the environment, linking identity to the system.
4. **Economic Participation**
   Trade and livelihood became intertwined with the structure.
5. **System Allegiance**
   Loyalty shifted as identity, provision, and relationships became dependent on the system.

The danger was not only idolatry, but it was also dependence. Are you Woke yet?

Once worship and livelihood intertwine, separation carries a cost. And whatever becomes costly to leave becomes powerful enough to control.

This same pattern appears in Revelation:

"The merchants of the earth are waxed rich through the abundance of her delicacies."
— ***Revelation 18:3 KJV***

Idolatrous systems never remain confined to temples. They expand into the marketplace, binding communities through both devotion and prosperity.

The Psychological Path into Compromise

The events at Baal-Peor reveal that compromise is rarely immediate—it is progressive.

Curiosity initiates exposure.
Exposure produces attraction.
Attraction normalizes participation.
Normalization weakens resistance.

The mind adapts to repeated environments. What once appeared dangerous begins to appear ordinary. By the time open rebellion appears, the internal resistance has already been dismantled.

The serpent does not command rebellion—he engineers conditions that make it appear harmless.

This is why as a believer we must know the word of God to be able to discern the difference between good and evil.

"But strong meat belongeth to them that are of full age, even those who by reason of use have their senses exercised to discern both good and evil."
— **Hebrews 5:14 KJV**

Corporate Consequence and Divine Judgment

The compromise at Baal-Peor soon affected the entire nation What began as individual participation spread through the community and altered the spiritual atmosphere of Isreal.

"And the anger of the LORD was kindled against Israel."
— Numbers 25:3 KJV

A plague spread through the camp, demonstrating that covenant violation carries communal impact. What begins privately affects atmospheres publicly.

Covenant communities are never spiritually neutral environments. Alignment or compromise within individuals influences the whole body. You must choose who you will serve. The heart determines where your worship lye. **(Mark 7:21-23)**

Phinehas and the Restoration of Covenant Zeal

In the midst of corruption, Phinehas acted with decisive zeal for the Lord's covenant.

"Phinehas... hath turned my wrath away from the children of Israel, while he was zealous for my sake among them."
— Numbers 25:11 KJV

His action interrupted the spread of compromise and restored clarity to Israel's allegiance. The plague ceased, and God established a covenant of peace with him.

Renewal often begins with individuals who refuse to normalize compromise when it threatens the integrity of a community. His boldness reminds us that a standard must be in place to honor the Lord. When this is done God's mercy and protection can be extended. In every generation there are those who refuse to tolerate what erodes truth, we must stand against the lies of deception. We cannot be passive while this type of strategy is still at play today. Jesus confronted a similar example of this in ***Matthew 21:12*** where they normalized it as being holy. Christ dealt with the deeper issue, the condition of the heart. His zeal was not only corrective but redemptive, restoring access to God not through rituals, but through Himself. The pattern is the same when covenant is threatened, restoration requires clarity, conviction and the courage to confront what has been accepted but not aligned with the word of Truth.

The Doctrine of Balaam in the Last Days

The warning Jesus gave in Revelation shows that Balaam's strategy did not disappear with ancient Israel. The same pattern appears wherever covenant communities encounter surrounding cultures and systems.

The doctrine of Balaam operates through cunning persuasion rather than open hostility. It encourages participation in environments that gradually weaken allegiance to God. It persuades people that engagement with surrounding systems will not affect their loyalty.

Yet the pattern remains the same: small compromises accumulate until identity shifts.

Christ calls His people to discernment and repentance so that covenant loyalty remains central.

Modern Insight

Seduction in a Contemporary System

The strategy of Balaam did not end in Moab; it has been refined.

Today, Baal-Peor no longer appears as an ancient idol, yet its structure remains intact. The system still merges pleasure, identity, and belonging into one environment. It simply wears different clothing. It appears in platforms, relationships, and cultures that normalize what God has already exposed. It invites participation before requiring conviction. It builds attachment before exposing allegiance. What once looked like temple feasts now looks like social environments where compromise is celebrated and conviction is silenced.

The pattern has not changed:

- Exposure becomes acceptance
- Acceptance becomes participation
- Participation becomes identity

Many do not fall because they reject God. They fall because they slowly adjust to the environments that no longer reflect Him. This is why discernment is not optional—it is survival.

"But strong meat belongeth to them that are of full age... who by reason of use have their senses exercised to discern both good and evil."
— Hebrews 5:14 KJV

Discernment must be exercised because seduction is cunning which is deceptive. The danger in this generation is not open rebellion—it is quiet agreement.

Agreement with what is entertained.
Agreement with what is normalized.
Agreement with what no longer convicts.

And over time, what is agreed with begins to shape what is desired.

Revelation Insight

Seduction and the Architecture of Compromise

The events surrounding Balaam reveal more than history; they expose a pattern. When the enemy cannot defeat a covenant people through direct opposition, he introduces systems that reshape allegiance gradually. At Bel-Peor, seduction was disguised as cultural celebration. Participation did not appear as rebellion; it appeared as belonging. What was presented as a connection slowly redefined the boundaries, making what was once separate feel acceptable. As involvement increased, discernment weakened, and what began as exposure moved toward participation without hesitation. In time, what was tolerated became normalized, and what was normalized no longer felt like compromise. This is how allegiance shifts—not through confrontation, but through subtle acceptance that reshapes what is considered right.

This is how systems expand.

Emotional engagement becomes relational integration.
Relational integration becomes economic participation.
Economic participation becomes allegiance and honor.

The book of Revelation exposes this same architecture on a global scale:

"For all nations have drunk of the wine of the wrath of her fornication... and the merchants of the earth are waxed rich through the abundance of her delicacies."
— Revelation 18:3 KJV

Here, worship and commerce merge. This reveals the deeper strategy: Idolatry expands into identity, culture, and economy. Once allegiance is tied to livelihood, separation becomes costly—and what is costly to leave becomes difficult to discern.

The story of Balaam therefore stands as an early exposure of a pattern that continues throughout history.

Seduction weakens allegiance before judgment exposes the corruption it produced.

Christ confronts this strategy by restoring the centrality of covenant loyalty. His call to repentance in Revelation reminds the Church that devotion to God cannot coexist with participation in systems that redefine allegiance.

Where obedience remains central, the strategy of Balaam fails. Where covenant loyalty is preserved, the seductive power of Babylon loses its influence.

CHAPTER NINE

Babylon, the Golden Age Illusion, and the Corporate Manipulation of the Mind

From Baal-Peor to Babylon: The Expansion of the System

The events at Baal-Peor exposed a strategy the enemy used against Israel. When Balaam could not curse the covenant people, he introduced a system that persuaded them to compromise their allegiance. Seduction replaced confrontation, and the people participated in practices that weakened their covenant alignment from within. This reveals a governing pattern.

When direct attack fails, systemic influence begins.

Yet Baal-Peor was not the final expression of that strategy. It was a localized demonstration of a pattern that appears throughout Scripture. What began as a system used to corrupt a single nation later appears on a much larger scale in the biblical portrayal of Babylon.

Where Baal-Peor seduced a community, The Babylon system seduces civilizations.

The serpent's strategy expands in scope as it matures. It begins by influencing individuals, then communities, and eventually entire societies. What was once a localized religious environment becomes a cultural, psychological, and economic architecture capable of reshaping identity of the nation.

To understand Babylon, therefore, one must recognize that it represents more than a historical empire. Babylon reveals a recurring pattern in which power, prosperity, and influence are woven together in ways that redirect allegiance away from God.

This is why Jesus said:

"Render therefore unto Caesar the things which are Caesar's; and unto God the things that are God's."
— Matthew 22:21 KJV

Ask yourself this question? Where is my allegiance?

The Origin of Babylon: Unity Without Submission

Genesis 11

The first appearance of Babylon's pattern occurs in the account of the Tower of Babel.

"And they said, Go to, let us build us a city and a tower... and let us make us a name."
— Genesis 11:4

The people of the earth possessed a single language and a shared purpose. Their unity was not disorganized, it was structured. Yet the objective of their unity revealed the spiritual danger beneath it. They desired to establish their own name rather than honor the authority of God.

"For all that is in the world, the lust of the flesh,and the lust of the eyes and the pride of life, is not of the Father, but is of the world."
— 1 John 2:16 KJV

The tower represented more than architectural ambition. It symbolized a civilization seeking identity and security apart from divine submission. Humanity attempted to build a structure that elevated its own achievements as the basis of its identity.

The Lord intervened by confusing their language and scattering them across the earth. This act was not simply judgment; it was restraint. Without that intervention, the consolidation of human pride could have produced a system powerful enough to deepen rebellion across the world. From the beginning, Babylon's defining characteristic was **power organized without reverence**

The Maturation of Babylon: When Success Becomes Identity

Daniel 4

Centuries later the same pattern emerged in the empire of Babylon under Nebuchadnezzar. The kingdom flourished with military strength, economic stability, and impressive infrastructure. Yet the prosperity of the empire gradually altered the king's perception of its source.

Standing within his royal palace, Nebuchadnezzar declared:

"Is not this great Babylon, that I have built for the house of the kingdom by the might of my power?"
— **Daniel 4:30 KJV**

In that moment the shift from gratitude to ownership became visible. What had been permitted by God was now claimed as the achievement of the king himself.

The narrative reveals how corporate pride forms. When success continues long enough, it produces confidence. Confidence can quietly evolve into self-reliance. Self-reliance then becomes the foundation for identity. **Pride** is the craftiness of the serpent to get you to worship in flesh and not submit to the leading of God's Spirit. Nebuchadnezzar's humbling demonstrated that power cannot secure permanence when it replaces reverence.

The empire he celebrated as his own achievement existed only by the permission of God. Babylon therefore illustrates a critical principle:

When success becomes identity, humility disappears.

The Golden Age Illusion

"Say not thou, what is the cause that the former days were better than these? for thou dost not enquire wisely concerning this."
— **Ecclesiastes 7:10 KJV**

One of Babylon's most effective psychological influences is the creation of what may be called the Golden Age illusion. This illusion forms when a civilization remembers its era of greatest strength and interprets that era as proof of its moral superiority.

History begins to reshape the perception. The period of expansion becomes the standard against which every other generation is measured. Economic growth, cultural influence, and political dominance are remembered as evidence that society must have been aligned with righteousness.

Over time, the memory of prosperity becomes a moral benchmark rather than seeking God first.

"But seek ye first the kingdom of God, and his righteousness; and all these things shall be added unto you."
— **Matthew 6:33 KJV**

When decline or instability later appears, the society assumes that righteousness has been lost because power has been lost. Instead of examining whether obedience to God weakened during prosperity, the culture longs for the restoration of dominance.

The Golden Age illusion therefore replaces repentance with nostalgia.

Rather than asking where covenant loyalty has drifted, the people become convinced that their greatest expansion must have been their purest moment. Scripture consistently challenges this assumption. Israel experienced periods of prosperity while injustice and idolatry flourished beneath the surface. The prophets confronted these conditions precisely because prosperity can conceal spiritual decline. The serpent's strategy thrives in such moments. When success is treated as proof of righteousness, self-examination disappears.

Babylon as a System of Worship and Commerce

"They that will be rich fall into temptation and a snare..."
— 1 Timothy 6:9 KJV

Babylon's influence does not remain confined to political authority. Like Baal-Peor before it, Babylon intertwines spiritual seduction with economic participation. Worship and commerce become inseparable parts of the same structure. The book of Revelation describes Babylon in language that highlights this union.

"The merchants of the earth are waxed rich through the abundance of her delicacies."
— Revelation 18:3 KJV

In Babylon the pursuit of prosperity becomes entangled with the values promoted by the system. Kings seek alliances within it, merchants gain wealth through it, and nations adopt its culture.

When economic advantage is connected to participation in a system, allegiance becomes profitable. Individuals and societies begin defending the structure because their prosperity depends on it.

This is why Babylon exerts such powerful influence. It offers not only identity but also opportunity. The system rewards participation and discourages separation.

As with Baal-Peor, the danger lies not merely in belief but in dependence.

"By the multitude of thy merchandise they have filled the midst of thee with violence..."
— **Ezekiel 28:16 KJV**

The Manipulation of the Corporate Mind

Babylon's strength lies in its ability to shape the thinking of entire populations. Over time, repeated participation in its systems alters the way societies evaluate success and security.

Several shifts occur in the corporate mind:

1. **Power becomes evidence of righteousness.**
   Dominance is interpreted as moral validation.
2. **Prosperity becomes evidence of favor.**
   Wealth is treated as proof that the system is correct.
3. **Influence becomes evidence of legitimacy.**
   Cultural authority replaces covenant obedience as the measure of success.

When these beliefs become widely accepted, questioning the system feels dangerous. Loyalty to the structure becomes intertwined with national identity.

This psychological influence explains why Babylon's fall in Revelation produces such mourning among kings and merchants. Their grief is not merely political or economic; it is existential.

The collapse of the system threatens the identity they built within it.

Christ and the Rejection of Babylon's Standard

Christ confronted the same pattern during His temptation in the wilderness. The adversary offered Him authority over the kingdoms of the world without the path of obedience and sacrifice.

"All these things will I give thee, if thou wilt fall down and worship me."
— *Matthew 4:9 KJV*

The offer represented Babylon's logic in its purest form, power without submission. Christ rejected the offer with a declaration that restores the proper order of allegiance.

"Thou shalt worship the Lord thy God, and him only shalt thou serve."
— *Matthew 4:10 KJV*

His refusal exposed the illusion that power or influence can replace obedience. The Kingdom of God is not built upon dominance but upon covenant loyalty.

Revelation Insight

The System Behind the Seduction

The account of Balaam and Baal-Peor reveals the beginning of a strategy that later appears on a global scale in the biblical description of Babylon. In both cases the enemy does not begin with open hostility. He introduces environments that slowly reshape allegiance.

At Baal-Peor the strategy was local and relational. Israel encountered a system where celebration, ritual sacrifice, and sensual attraction blended together. Participation began through social interaction and progressed into spiritual compromise. The covenant people were not conquered by force; they were drawn into a structure that weakened their devotion from within.

Babylon represents the expansion of that same pattern. What appeared locally at Baal-Peor becomes international in Revelation. Worship, culture, and commerce unite to form a structure that influences entire civilizations.

"For all nations have drunk of the wine of the wrath of her fornication... and the merchants of the earth are waxed rich through the abundance of her delicacies."
— ***Revelation 18:3 KJV***

The language of fornication describes spiritual unfaithfulness, yet the passage also emphasizes wealth and trade. Babylon does not operate only through religion. It binds people through prosperity, identity, and cultural influence. Participation becomes attractive because it appears beneficial.

This reveals the deeper pattern behind the serpent's strategy. Idolatry rarely remains confined to belief alone. It grows through systems that shape celebration, relationships, economics, and national identity. When those systems mature, allegiance shifts quietly from covenant obedience to participation in the structure itself.

The danger is not merely external influence but internal agreement. People may continue to speak the language of faith while their values and loyalties are slowly being shaped by the surrounding system.

Christ confronts this pattern by restoring the foundation of allegiance. His Kingdom is not built upon the structures of Babylon or the seductions of prosperity. It is established through obedience to the Father and loyalty to His covenant.

Where Christ remains the center of identity, the seduction of Babylon loses its authority. A people who measure success by faithfulness rather than power is not easily absorbed into the systems that once captured nations.

Yet the warning of Scripture remains clear. Seduction rarely announces itself as rebellion. It presents itself as opportunity, celebration, or progress. When prosperity, culture, and identity become intertwined with systems that draw the heart away from covenant obedience, allegiance begins to shift quietly.

For this reason, the people of God must remain discerning. The question is not only what a system produces, but what it requires of the heart. Any structure that slowly replaces devotion to God with devotion to its own success carries the same pattern revealed at Baal-Peor and later perfected in Babylon.

Christ calls His people to recognize these patterns and remain faithful. Where covenant loyalty remains central, the seductive architecture of Babylon loses its hold. Rebuilding threatens systems that profit from captivity. The opposition was not random—it was strategic. If Jerusalem was restored, control would be broken. If the walls were rebuilt, dependence would end. What the enemy fears most is not deliverance alone, but restoration that removes his access.

"Be it known now unto the king, that, if this city be builded, and the walls set up again, then will they not pay toll, tribute, and custom, and so thou shalt endamage the revenue of the kings."

— Ezra 4:13 KJV

CHAPTER TEN

2 Kings 17 – The Anatomy of a Fallen Nation

The collapse of Israel did not occur in a single moment. Nations rarely fall suddenly, nor do they collapse without warning. Their downfall begins long before the visible crisis appears. Long before armies invade or borders give way, something far more dangerous is already unfolding beneath the surface. The foundations that once anchored a people begin to erode quietly and progressively. Values begin to shift, loyalties are subtly redirected, and what was once unthinkable gradually becomes normalized.

Second Kings chapter seventeen records the exile of the northern kingdom of Israel by the Assyrian Empire. Yet before describing the fall itself, the Scripture pauses intentionally to explain the deeper reason behind it. What follows is one of the most revealing passages in the Bible concerning the spiritual decline of a nation. It reads almost like a diagnosis from God Himself, exposing the internal conditions that made Israel's collapse not only possible, but inevitable.

The chapter begins by reminding the reader of Israel's original identity. These were the people whom God had delivered from Egypt. They were the nation who had witnessed His power in the wilderness, who had received the covenant at Sinai, and who had been warned repeatedly through the prophets to remain faithful.

Yet the text reveals that something had shifted within the heart of the nation.

"For so it was, that the children of Israel had sinned against the LORD their God... and had feared other gods."
— 2 Kings 17:7 KJV

The first step in Israel's decline was not military weakness, nor was it economic instability. It was misplaced fear. Fear determines where your allegiance is. What people fear ultimately reveals what they trust, and what they trust will always shape their decisions. When Israel began to fear other gods, their loyalty had already begun to shift, even before their behavior fully reflected it.

Israel slowly began to adopt the customs of the surrounding nations. These customs appeared attractive because they promised stability, prosperity, and cultural acceptance. Yet each practice carried within it in a crafty but powerful redirection of loyalty.

The text then describes a progression of compromise that reveals just how deeply the nation had drifted.

• They walked in the statutes of the surrounding nations.
• They built high places throughout the land.
• They established sacred pillars and groves.
• They practiced rituals connected to foreign gods.

These practices were not introduced overnight. They were added gradually, often justified as harmless adaptations to cultural realities or necessary adjustments to changing circumstances. Over time, however, they reshaped the entire spiritual landscape of the nation.

The Scripture then explains the deeper issue beneath the behavior.

"They rejected his statutes, and his covenant that he made with their fathers... and they followed vanity and became vain."
— 2 Kings 17:15 KJV

The phrase *"followed vanity and became vain"* describes more than moral weakness. It reveals a transformation of identity. When Israel began to imitate the surrounding nations, they adopted systems that appeared successful but were empty of covenant substance. What they pursued did not remain external—it became internal.

What they followed eventually shaped who they became.

This principle remains true for every generation:
A people will eventually become like the systems they consistently imitate.

The chapter continues to list the practices that had taken root in the land.

• They worshipped the host of heaven.
• They served Baal.
• They practiced divination and enchantments.
• They sacrificed their sons and daughters in the fire.

Each practice represented another step away from covenant loyalty and a deeper integration into foreign systems of worship. These systems were not simply religious rituals; they were cultural structures that shaped thinking, behavior, perception, and identity.

Yet the most revealing statement in the entire chapter appears later in the text.

"They feared the LORD and served their own gods."
— 2 Kings 17:33 KJV

This sentence exposes the heart of Israel's downfall. They did not completely abandon the Lord. Instead, they attempted to combine covenant faith with the systems of surrounding cultures. They believed they could maintain devotion to God while also participating in practices that directly contradicted His commands. We see this in the world today.

This is the danger of Compromise.

Contamination allows people to believe they remain faithful while their allegiance is slowly being redirected. It creates the illusion of devotion while hollowing out the foundation of covenant truth. Outwardly, everything appears intact—but inwardly, the structure is weakening.

Over time, the consequences of this condition became unavoidable.

"Therefore the LORD was very angry with Israel, and removed them out of his sight."
— 2 Kings 17:18 KJV

Israel was carried into exile. The nation that had once been delivered from Egypt now found itself displaced—not because God had failed, but because they had gradually exchanged covenant loyalty for cultural imitation.

The tragedy of Israel's fall is not only historical—it is deeply instructional. This chapter reveals how easily people can drift when they allow external systems to redefine their identity.

Modern Insight

The Same Pattern Today

This pattern has not disappeared, it has evolved.

Today, believers are not building high places on hills, but they are building platforms in their lives where other systems are given influence alongside God. The shift still begins the same way, with misplaced fear.

• Fear of lack leads people to trust money over God.
• Fear of rejection leads people to conform to culture over truth.
• Fear of uncertainty leads people to seek control instead of surrender.

Modern *"customs of the nations*" do not always look like idols—they look like normal life. They show up as:

• Systems that prioritize success over obedience
• Cultures that normalize compromise in the name of acceptance

• Mindsets that value feelings over truth
• Spiritual practices that seek results without relationship

Just like Israel, these things are rarely introduced as rebellion. They are introduced as reasonable, helpful, or even necessary.

What begins as participation becomes normalization.
What becomes normalization becomes identity.

The same progression still exists:

• Exposure → Acceptance → Participation → Identity

"This people draweth nigh unto me with their mouth, and honoureth me with their lips; but their heart is far from me."
— Matthew 15:8 KJV

And just like Israel, many believers today live in a form of mixture.
They acknowledge God but are shaped by the culture of the world.
They confess truth but follow the systems that contradict it.
They maintain faith outwardly, while inwardly aligning with other influences.

This is why the warning remains relevant. Mixture does not destroy immediately—it reshapes gradually. And the question for every generation is the same.

What is forming your thinking—covenant truth or surrounding systems?

Because whatever you consistently follow, you will eventually become.

"Wherefore the Lord said, Forasmuch as this people draw near me with their mouth, and with their lips do honour me, but have removed their heart far from me..."

— Isaiah 29:13 KJV

The Foreign Gods of Samaria

Understanding the Cultures Behind the Idols

When Assyria conquered the northern kingdom of Israel, they followed a political strategy common in the ancient world. Conquered peoples were removed from their homeland and replaced with settlers from other territories. This prevented rebellion and diluted national identity.

The Scripture records this population transfer clearly.

"And the king of Assyria brought men from Babylon, and from Cuthah, and from Ava, and from Hamath, and from Sepharvaim, and placed them in the cities of Samaria."
— 2 Kings 17:24 KJV

These settlers brought more than their belongings. They brought their **religions, gods, rituals, and cultural systems**. Each god represented the worldview of the people who worshiped it.

The result was a land filled with **competing religious systems**, all operating side by side.

The People of Babylon – Succoth-benoth

Babylon was one of the most influential civilizations of the ancient world. Their religion was complex and organized around a large pantheon of gods connected to fertility, the stars, agriculture, and prosperity. Succoth-benoth appears to be associated with fertility worship and is often linked with the broader Babylonian cult of **Ishtar**, the goddess connected with sexuality, fertility, and prosperity. Fertility cults were not simply about reproduction.

They were tied to **economic prosperity and agricultural success**. Rituals were believed to influence the productivity of the land and the growth of families.

In these systems, prosperity could be managed through ritual performance rather than covenant obedience.

The biblical writers saw this as a distortion of worship because it shifted trust from God to **ritual systems promising prosperity**.

The People of Cuthah – Nergal

The settlers from **Cuthah** brought the worship of **Nergal**, one of the more feared deities of Mesopotamia.

Nergal was associated with:

- war
- plague
- death
- the underworld

In ancient texts he appears as a god connected with destruction and disease. His cult reflected the belief that forces of death and catastrophe needed to be appeased.

When societies center their worldview around fear of destructive power, violence itself begins to appear sacred.

The worship of Nergal reveals how cultures can elevate **force and domination as ultimate authority**.

The People of Hamath – Ashima

The settlers from **Hamath**, a Syrian city-state north of Israel, worshiped **Ashima**.

Historical sources suggest Ashima functioned as a regional or tribal deity associated with the protection of the community. Worship of such gods reinforced **shared identity and cultural loyalty**.

In many ancient societies religion and national identity were inseparable. Loyalty to the god of the land meant loyalty to the culture of the land.

This is why the prophets continually warned Israel against adopting the religious practices of surrounding nations.

When religious systems are tied to cultural identity, abandoning them can feel like abandoning one's people.

The Avites – Nibhaz and Tartak

Another group mentioned in the text were the **Avites**, who brought with them the worship of **Nibhaz and Tartak**.

Ancient writers describe these deities as animal-form gods. Animal symbolism was extremely common in ancient religions.

Animals represented strength, fertility, protection, or mythological forces believed to influence the natural world.

These cults reflect the way early societies explained the world through symbolic mythologies that shaped how people understood nature and power.

The People of Sepharvaim –

Adrammelech and Anammelech

The settlers from **Sepharvaim**, likely located along the Euphrates River, worshiped **Adrammelech and Anammelech**.

The Scripture records something particularly disturbing about their worship.

"The Sepharvites burnt their children in fire to Adrammelech and Anammelech."
— 2 Kings 17:31 KJV

Child sacrifice was practiced in several ancient cultures during times of crisis. It was believed that offering the most precious thing one possessed would secure divine favor or avert disaster.

The Bible condemns this practice repeatedly because it represents the extreme distortion of worship. Instead of trusting God, people attempted to manipulate divine power through the ultimate sacrifice.

The Spiritual Problem – Mixture

After listing the gods and cultures present in Samaria, the text reveals the central issue.

"They feared the LORD and served their own gods."
— 2 Kings 17:33 KJV

This single sentence exposes the spiritual problem of the chapter.

The people did not completely reject the LORD. Instead, they **combined covenant faith with foreign systems of worship**.

This blending of belief systems is called **syncretism**.

Syncretism allows people to maintain the appearance of devotion while their loyalty is gradually redirected.

This chapter explains that this mixture continued for generations.

"So these nations feared the LORD, and served their graven images, both their children, and their children's children."
— 2 Kings 17:41 KJV

The warning of the passage is therefore clear. The greatest threat to covenant identity is not always open rebellion but **the gradual blending of competing systems of belief**.

After Assyria moved these different people into Samaria, something unusual happened. The text says that the new settlers did not initially know how to worship the LORD, and lions began attacking them.

"And so it was at the beginning of their dwelling there, that they feared not the LORD: therefore the LORD sent lions among them, which slew some of them."
— 2 Kings 17:25 KJV

The Assyrian king then sent an Israelite priest back to teach them the worship of the God of the land.

"Carry thither one of the priests whom ye brought from thence... and let them teach them the manner of the God of the land."
— 2 Kings 17:27 KJV

This created a strange religious situation.

The new inhabitants learned about the LORD from the priest, yet they **kept the worship of their own gods**.

"Howbeit every nation made gods of their own, and put them in the houses of the high places."
— 2 Kings 17:29 KJV

The result was a society where multiple religious systems existed together. The people acknowledged the LORD but continued honoring their traditional deities.

Scripture summarizes the situation with a statement that appears several times in the chapter:

"They feared the LORD and served their own gods."
— 2 Kings 17:33

This reveals the heart of the problem. The issue was not simply that foreign gods were present. The deeper issue was **divided allegiance**. The people attempted to combine the worship of the LORD with the religious traditions of their own cultures.

"So these nations feared the LORD, and served their graven images, both their children, and their children's children: as did their fathers, so do they unto this day."
— 2 Kings 17:41 KJV

This type of compromise rarely remains temporary. Once it becomes normal, it is passed down through inherited cultural traditions, making it more difficult to recognize to what shifted in loyalty.

Over time, what was introduced becomes embedded, and never questioned. In this way, allegiance is no longer examined, it is assumed to be a part of being normal.

Modern Insight –Recognizing Today's "Foreign God's

The gods of Samaria may seem distant, but their patterns are not. The names have changed, the altars look different, and the rituals are more deceitful—but the systems remain.

Foreign gods today are not always statues—they are **systems of trust, identity, and control that compete with God for influence over the heart**.

The same categories seen in Samaria still exist, only now they are internalized, normalized, and often honored and celebrated.

Modern Succoth-benoth – Prosperity Without Covenant

Where ancient systems promised fertility and increase, modern culture promises same fertility, success, wealth, and influence often without surrender to God.

This appears as:

- Trusting financial systems more than God's provision
- Measuring worth by productivity, income, or status
- Pursuing abundance without obedience even Invitro fertility trust in placing trust in human ability over God's original design.

The question is no longer, "Do you worship a fertility god?"
It becomes: **What or who do you believe is your source?**

"But thou shalt remember the LORD thy God: for it is he that giveth thee power to get wealth."
— Deuteronomy 8:18 KJV

When prosperity becomes the goal instead of the byproduct of obedience, a foreign system has already taken root. When prosperity becomes the goal instead of obedience this leads to deception, a strategy of the serpent. What once required alters now operate through dependence, shaping trust, redefining provision and quietly shifting the reliance from God to systems of man. The danger is not always visible, because increase can still occur, but the source has been exchanged. What appears to be a blessing, actually is independence wrapped in deceit. And when dependence on God is replaced, covenant is no longer the foundation, control dominating.

Modern Nergal – Fear, Control, and Survival Thinking

Where Nergal represented death, destruction, and fear, modern systems are driven by anxiety, control, and survival.

This appears as:

• Living in constant fear of loss, failure, or instability
• Making decisions based on worst-case outcomes instead of faith
• Trusting control more than surrender

Fear becomes the governing force.

"The fear of man bringeth a snare..."
— ***Proverbs 29:25 KJV***

When fear becomes the voice you obey, it has already become the god you serve.

Modern Ashima – Identity Rooted in Culture, Not Covenant

Ashima represented tribal identity and cultural belonging. Today, identity is often shaped more by culture than by Christ.

This appears as:

• Defining yourself by background, experience, or community instead of God's Word
• Aligning beliefs with cultural expectations instead of Scripture
• Feeling pressure to conform in order to belong

"Be not conformed to this world..."
— ***Romans 12:2 KJV***

When identity is formed by culture instead of covenant, allegiance has already shifted. In today's landscape, social trends, group affiliations political identities often carry more weight than God's call. Many feel compelled to adjust convictions just to fit into societal norms. Instead of asking, "Who does God say I am?" the question becomes, "How do I fit into the crowd?" The more we seek acceptance from the world's narratives, the less we hear god's voice shaping us.

True identity is found when we return to the source, Christ, who defines who we are, regardless of cultures shift.

Modern Nibhaz & Tartak – Living by Instinct Instead of Truth

Nibhaz and Tartak were associated with forms that reflected animalistic nature—systems that emphasized instinct, impulse, and natural drive. These were not centered on truth or covenant, but on behavior shaped by what felt natural rather than what was revealed by God.

The system trained people to follow impulse instead of instruction.

What God designed to be governed by His Word—thought, behavior, and desire—was instead surrendered to instinct.

Discipline was replaced with reaction, and truth was replaced with what felt immediate and natural.

This deception remains present in modern form. Identity and behavior are often shaped by impulse rather than truth. People are encouraged to *"follow their feelings,"* "trust their instincts," and "*live authentically*," even when those instincts are not aligned with God.

This appears as:

- making decisions based on feelings rather than Scripture
- justifying behavior because it feels natural
- rejecting correction in favor of self-expression
- elevating instinct above obedience

Scripture gives a direct contrast:

"The heart is deceitful above all things, and desperately wicked: who can know it?"
— Jeremiah 17:9 KJV

What feels right is not always true. When instinct becomes the guide, truth is no longer the authority. The mind is no longer renewed. What should be brought into submission is instead followed without question.

"Casting down imaginations... and bringing into captivity every thought to the obedience of Christ."
— 2 Corinthians 10:5 KJV

Scripture calls you as a believer to a different standard—not to be led by the flesh, but to be transformed by the renewing of the mind.

"He that trusteth in his own heart is a fool..."
— Proverbs 28:26 KJV

When instinct replaces instruction, the soul becomes its own authority.

Modern Adrammelech & Anammelech – Sacrifice for Success

Child sacrifice may seem extreme, but the principle still exists—sacrificing what matters most for gain.

This appears as:

• Abortions to preserve lifestyle and avoid responsibility and maintain financial or relational stability

• Forcing them into sports, academics, or platforms for status

• Education systems redefining truth and morality
• Cultural ideologies replacing biblical identity

"And they have built the high places of Tophet... to burn their sons and their daughters in the fire, which I commanded them not, neither came it into my heart."
— Jeremiah 7:31 KJV

"They sacrificed their sons and their daughters unto devils,
And shed innocent blood... and the land was polluted with blood."
— Psalm 106:37–38 KJV

Are willing to sacrifice **what God gave you** in order to gain something He did not ask for…has it already become an altar.

In ancient fires it consumed the bodies. In modern fires it consumes identity, purpose, and destiny, but the call of God has not changed:

Children are not sacrifices they are stewardship a gift from the LORD.

You must understand when we operate outside of the blueprint of the Lord it becomes an Ishmeal instead of Issac the Promise...

The Mirror: Where This Becomes Personal

The danger is not that these systems exist.
The danger is when they exist **within the believer's life without being discerned**.

Just like in Samaria,

"They feared the LORD and served their own gods."
— 2 Kings 17:33 KJV

This is the modern condition of mixture:

• Loving God but trusting systems
• Confessing truth but living by culture
• Praying on Sunday but governed by fear on Monday

"This people draweth nigh unto me with their mouth... but their heart is far from me."
— Matthew 15:8 KJV

This is where the reader must pause—not to analyze history, but to examine alignment.

Heart Check Questions (Conviction, Not Condemnation)

• What do I run to first—God or a system?
• What influences my decisions more—faith or fear?
• What defines me—Scripture or culture?
• What am I unwilling to surrender?

Because whatever answers those questions are shaping your worship.

Revelation Insight

Foreign gods are not always chosen; they are often a fascination.

They enter through exposure, agreement, and repetition until they feel normal.

But what feels normal is not always righteous.
And what is common is not always covenant.

God is not asking for partial allegiance.

"Thou shalt have no other gods before me."
— Exodus 20:3 KJV

— Not beside Him.
— Not alongside Him.
— Not hidden within Him.

"For I am persuaded, that neither death, nor life, nor angels, nor principalities, nor powers, nor things present, nor things to come, Nor height, nor depth, nor any other creature, shall be able to separate us from the love of God, which is in Christ Jesus our Lord."
— Romans 8:38–39 KJV

When Mixture Becomes Infrastructure

Second **Kings 17** does not just reveal compromise—it reveals what happens when compromise becomes established.

What began as individual disobedience in Israel did not remain personal. It became structured, normalized, and eventually inherited. By the time Assyria repopulated the land, mixture was no longer an issue of isolated choice, it had become embedded into the environment itself.

The new inhabitants of Samaria did not create the situation they stepped into it.

"They feared the LORD and served their own gods."
— 2 Kings 17:33 KJV

This was no longer a struggle of decision—it was a condition of the system.

The false priest and prophets then and today false priest, prophets, teachers, evangelists and apostles taught them and teach about the God of the land, yet the system they lived in allowed them to add

Him without surrendering anything else. **Same strategy**. This reveals a critical shift, when mingling combines, it no longer feels like compromise it feels like order.

The serpent's strategy at this level is no longer persuasion it is deceptive infrastructure.

Truth is no longer rejected, it is consumed, redefined, and placed alongside competing influences. In this state, people no longer feel conflicted because the system itself has removed the tension.

They do not feel divided.
They feel balanced and free of the delusion.

"And for this cause God shall send them strong delusion, that they should believe a lie That they all might be damned who believed not the truth but had pleasure in unrighteousness."
— 2 Thessalonians 2:11–12 KJV

But what appears as balance is actually the cunning deception that the serpent uses to blind the mind.

"In whom the god of this world hath blinded the minds of them which believe not, lest the light of the glorious gospel of Christ... should shine unto them."
— 2 Corinthians 4:4 KJV

This is how deception deepens.
Not by removing God—but by reducing Him.

In this condition:
- God is acknowledged but not obeyed fully Compromise set in.
- Truth is heard but filtered through other systems cannot hear God.
- Worship exists, but without exclusive allegiance.

Mixture at this stage becomes generational.

"So these nations feared the LORD and served their graven images... so do they unto this day."
— 2 Kings 17:41 KJV

What was once compromise becomes tradition.
What was once disobedience becomes culture.
What was once introduced becomes inherited.

This is the danger revealed in this chapter. A system can carry a form of God while removing His authority. Once that system is established, people no longer recognize it as disobedience, they recognize it as normal everyday life. Yet the call of God does not change. He does not call His people to coexistence; He calls them to consecration set apart. Until the system is confronted, the heart cannot fully return.

Because when disobedience becomes the way of life, repentance must go deeper than behavior, it must dismantle what has been built.

Wherefore come out from among them, and be ye separate, saith the Lord, and touch not the unclean thing..."
— 2 Corinthians 6:17 KJV

CHAPTER ELEVEN

Natural Principalities – The Systems Behind Nations

Daniel 10 and the Conflict Behind Empires

Throughout Scripture the rise and fall of nations is never presented as random history. Kingdoms appear, expand, dominate regions of the earth, and eventually disappear. Yet the Bible repeatedly reminds the reader that political history alone does not explain the full picture. Behind the visible structures of power there are deeper realities shaping the direction of societies.

Daniel chapter ten provides one of the clearest moments in Scripture where God allows a servant to glimpse this reality. The chapter does not attempt to map the unseen world, nor does it invite speculation about spiritual hierarchies. Instead, it reveals that the conflicts affecting nations can involve more than human decisions.

Daniel had been seeking the Lord with fasting and prayer. For twenty-one days he humbled himself before God, asking for understanding concerning the future of his people. When the heavenly messenger finally appeared, he explained something unexpected.

"Fear not, Daniel: for from the first day that thou didst set thine heart to understand... thy words were heard."
— Daniel 10:12 KJV

The prayer had been heard immediately.

Yet the messenger revealed that the answer had been delayed.

"But the prince of the kingdom of Persia withstood me one and twenty days."
— Daniel 10:13 KJV

Later another coming power is mentioned.

"And when I am gone forth, lo, the prince of Grecia shall come."
— Daniel 10:20 KJV

These verses reveal a principle that appears throughout Scripture: **nations operate within systems of influence that can extend beyond what is visible to human eyes.**

Nations as Systems of Power

When Daniel receives this revelation, the Persian Empire was the dominant power of the ancient world. Persia ruled vast territories stretching from Central Asia to the Mediterranean. Its influence shaped law, economics, trade, and governance throughout the region. Empires do more than control land. They create **systems**. A system includes the structures that organize society:

- laws
- political authority
- economic structures
- education
- religion
- culture

These structures gradually shape how people think about power, success, and identity. Persia was known for its administrative organization. The empire divided its territory into provinces governed by officials called satraps. These administrators collected taxes, enforced laws, and maintained the authority of the king throughout distant regions.

The strength of Persia did not lie only in military conquest. It lay in an **organized system of control**.

Greece – The System of Cultural Influence

After Persia came Greece.

While Persia governed through administration, Greece influenced the world through culture and intellect.

When Alexander the Great expanded the Greek empire, he spread Greek language, philosophy, art, and education throughout the Mediterranean world. Even after the empire fractured politically, Greek thought continued to shape how people understood politics, ethics, science, and human identity.

Greek philosophy emphasized human reasoning and intellectual pursuit. Schools such as Stoicism and Platonism attempted to explain the nature of truth, morality, and reality through philosophical systems.

Greece therefore represents a different kind of influence. Instead of controlling through administrative structures, Greece reshaped the world through **ideas**. Ideas can shape civilizations for centuries.

Natural Principalities and the Structure of Power

Daniel's vision reveals that behind powerful empires there can also be deeper influence affecting their direction. Scripture does not encourage believers to obsess over unseen forces. Instead, it reminds the reader that human history cannot always be understood by political analysis alone.

Empires become powerful because systems form around them.

These systems influence entire population through education, culture, economics, and law. Over time they shape how people think and what they believe about authority and prosperity.

This is why Scripture repeatedly warns God's people about the influence of surrounding systems.

"For we wrestle not against flesh and blood."
— Ephesians 6:12 KJV

The struggle described in Scripture is not primarily against other people. It involves the forces that shape the systems influencing societies.

The Psychology of Systems

One of the most powerful aspects of any empire is not merely its ability to enforce authority, but its ability to shape perception. Systems rarely dominate people through force alone; they influence them by quietly training the way they think. This influence is not immediate or aggressive, gradual, consistent, and often imperceptible.

A system does not need to control behavior directly if it can shape belief. Once belief is shaped, behavior will follow naturally.

Education plays a central role in this process. It does more than transfer information, it establishes what is considered true, valuable, and worth pursuing. Over time, what is taught becomes what is trusted. Economic structures reinforce this conditioning by defining what success looks like. They reward certain behaviors, elevate specific outcomes, and create a framework where value is measured according to the system's priorities.

Philosophy then gives language to these structures. It explains purpose, identity, and meaning in ways that align with the system's design. Religion, whether true or distorted, further reinforces these conclusions by shaping moral boundaries and spiritual understanding. Together, these influences create a unified framework through which reality is interpreted.

What begins as external influence eventually becomes internal agreement.

Over time, people no longer feel shaped by the system—they feel as though they are simply thinking for themselves. Yet their thoughts have already been filtered, trained, and aligned with the structures around them. What a society consistently rewards becomes desirable. What it consistently fears becomes controlling. What it consistently celebrates becomes identity.

This is how systems move from influence to ownership.

The danger is not always visible. People rarely recognize the moment when their thinking begins to shift. There is no clear line where influence becomes agreement. Instead, the transition happens quietly, through repetition and normalization, until what was once questioned is no longer examined.

Scripture speaks directly to this process:

"Take heed lest any man spoil you through philosophy and vain deceit, after the tradition of men, after the rudiments of the world, and not after Christ."
— Colossians 2:8 KJV

The warning is not simply against false teaching—it is against being shaped by systems that redefine truth apart from Christ. The word *spoil* suggests being carried away, taken captive without resistance. This captivity does not begin with action, it begins in thought.

"Wherefore gird up the loins of your mind, be sober, and hope to the end..."
— 1 Peter 1:13 KJV

A mind shaped by a system will defend that system, even when it contradicts the truth.

Again remember, influence has matured into allegiance at that point.

This is why the battle described in Scripture is not primarily externality. Before systems are resisted outwardly, they must be discerned inwardly. Before one's behavior changes, what is perceived must be confronted.

Once a system has shaped how a person sees, it has already begun to shape who they are.

Revelation Without Fascination

Daniel was allowed to see that the struggles affecting nations involve more than political decisions. Yet the vision stops there—not because there was nothing more to reveal, but because there was nothing more required.

He is not instructed to investigate the unseen world. He is not told to catalogue invisible rulers or develop theories about spiritual hierarchies. The revelation is given, but it is not expanded beyond its purpose.

The purpose of the revelation is discernment.

Daniel needed to understand that the moment in which he lived was not isolated. It was part of a much larger conflict affecting the direction of nations and the unfolding of God's plan. What he was experiencing had context beyond what was visible—but his assignment did not change because of it. This distinction is very essential. Revelation is given to produce clarity.

The believer's responsibility, therefore, remains unchanged: faithfulness, humility, and obedience to God. Insight into larger realities does not replace obedience in present responsibility.

It reinforces it.

The Stability of God's Kingdom

Persia rose and it fell but behind this you must understand was a demonic principality that controlled the narrative. Greece followed, gained power, and declined, and throughout history empires have repeated the same cycle, emerging, expanding, dominating, and then fading from the earth, because this is the nature of human systems, they are formed within limitation and sustained by what must continually be upheld. But the Kingdom of God does not move within this pattern, for it is not subject to time, nor does it depend on preservation to remain. As it is written, *"Thy kingdom is an everlasting kingdom, and thy dominion endureth throughout all generations." —**Psalm 145:13*** KJV. Earthly empires rely on military strength, political authority, and cultural influence to maintain their position, requiring constant reinforcement their power is stemmed from human effort, only the Kingdom of God is established through righteousness, truth, and obedience, and it stands because its foundation cannot be altered. *"For the kingdom of God is not in word, but in power." —**1 Corinthians 4:20 KJV**.* Where human systems are temporary and subject to collapse, the authority of God remains unchanging, untouched by the rise and fall of nations. What is built by deception must eventually confront its limits, but what is established by God endures, it is not sustained by unholy means, it is upheld by His nature. *"Jesus Christ the same yesterday, and today, and forever." —**Hebrews 13:8*** **KJV**. The structures of this world may appear stable and deeply rooted, yet anything formed outside of God's order carries within it the inability to survive, while the Kingdom of God does not shift, weaken, or decline. The Sword of the Spirit will bring forth death to every demonic system structured in the earth, for "*the word of God is quick, and powerful, and sharper than any two-edged sword." —**Hebrews 4:12 KJV**.*

"Wherefore we receiving a kingdom which cannot be moved, let us have grace." ***—Hebrews 12:28 KJV.***

This is the dividing line, one must be maintained, the other cannot be moved only what is rooted in the Kingdom of God will remain when all else is removed.

Revelation Insight– Systems Rise – Christ Reigns

Daniel 10 makes it plain that what operates through some human systems in the earth is not neutral; behind regions and orders there can be demonic principalities assigned to influence, reinforce, and preserve alignment against the truth of God. *The "prince of the kingdom of Persia"* is not presented as a human ruler, but as a spiritual authority working in connection with that kingdom, resisting what God had already released.

"from the first day that thou didst set thine heart to understand... thy words were heard"

—Daniel 10:12 KJV

yet "the prince of the kingdom of Persia withstood me one and twenty days."

—Daniel 10:13 KJV

This uncovers that demonic principalities can control what is established, when not governed with the presence of the Holy Spirit, they work to uphold systems through deception, agreement, and oppression so that what is misaligned continues to take rule.

Their function is to influence minds, shape culture, and stabilize structures that would otherwise collapse under the truth of the Holy Spirit, embedding themselves into patterns of thought and Character so that the system appears natural while being spiritually sustained. But their authority is limited. The resistance did not stop the answer; it only contended with its movement. No principality has the power to cancel what God has released. What they uphold must be continually reinforced it is not rooted in what is Holy and anything that must be sustained by demonic influence is already unstable at its core. God's rule stands outside and above every such structure,

"And in the days of these kings shall the God of heaven set up a kingdom, which shall never be destroyed." ***—Daniel 2:44*** **KJV.**

His Kingdom is not influenced, reinforced, or preserved by external means, it remains because it is established by Him.

Through Jesus Christ, the believer is not left under the authority of these demonic systems but is transferred out from under their rule, *"Who hath delivered us from the power of darkness, and hath translated us into the kingdom of his dear Son."*

—Colossians 1:13 KJV.

This is a real change of authority. It means that while demonic principalities may still operate within systems in the earth, they no longer have rightful authority over the one who belongs to Christ. Their influence can press, but it cannot define; it can attempt to re-shape, but it cannot establish identity or determine outcome.

CHAPTER TWELVE

Vows Born from Fear– How Wounded Identity Becomes a Door for Deception

Judges 11

The book of Judges captures a time in Israel's history marked by instability, spiritual confusion, and repeated cycles of compromise. The people had entered the land promised to Abraham, yet they had not fully removed the surrounding nations or the systems those nations carried out. As a result, Israel did not simply occupy territory—they lived immersed in competing definitions of worship, sacrifice, power, and identity.

Over time, the proximity became influence, and influence became internal agreement. Judges chapter eleven unfolds within this environment, and the story of Jephthah must be understood through both his personal history and the system surrounding him. It is often remembered for the vow he made before battle, yet the vow itself is not the beginning of the problem—it is the result of something deeper.

Jephthah is introduced as a man of strength marked by rejection.

"Now Jephthah the Gileadite was a mighty man of valour, and he was the son of an harlot."
— Judges 11:1 KJV

His identity is defined in tension—strength in function, rejection in origin. As the sons of Gilead matured, they expelled him from the household, denying him inheritance and belonging.

"Thou shalt not inherit in our father's house; for thou art the son of a strange woman."
— Judges 11:2 KJV

Rejection became the soil in which his identity developed. He was forced into the land of Tob, where he gathered men who, like himself, lived outside accepted structure. Long before he ever faced an external enemy, Jephthah had already been shaped internally by displacement and the need to establish worth without affirmation.

Years later, when the Ammonites rose against Israel, the elders of Gilead returned—not to restore relationship, but to recruit strength. The man they rejected became the man they needed.

Jephthah's response exposes the enduring nature of rejection.

"*Did not ye hate me, and expel me out of my father's house?"*
— ***Judges 11:7 KJV***

Their offer was simple: fight for us, and you will become our head.

What they offered externally touched something unresolved internally. Leadership was no longer just an assignment, it became validation. In that moment, the opportunity to lead carried more than responsibility; it carried the weight of proving identity.

The System Behind the Decision

Before the battle, Jephthah demonstrated that he understood Israel's history. He attempted to reason with the king of Ammon, recounting how God had given the land to His people. His knowledge was accurate, yet his perception of God had already been influenced by the surrounding systems.

The cultures around Israel operated on transactional worship. Their gods were believed to respond to sacrifice according to its magnitude. The greater the offering, the greater the response. Favor was negotiated. Victory was secured through exchange.

In its most extreme form, this system justified human sacrifice.

God explicitly rejected this framework:

"Thou shalt not do so unto the LORD thy God... for even their sons and their daughters they have burnt in the fire to their gods."
— Deuteronomy 12:31 KJV

The God of Israel does not respond to bargains. He establishes covenant. Yet exposure to a system, over time, reshapes perception even when truth is known.

The Strategy Beneath the Surface

What unfolds next reveals not just a mistake, but a pattern. The serpent does not begin by attacking strength—he begins by studying wounds. He does not first distort behavior—he distorts perception through pressure.

The strategy operating in Jephthah's life can be seen clearly:

1. Identity Wound
Rejection shaped how Jephthah saw himself.

2. Validation Pressure
Leadership became an opportunity to prove worth.

3. Cultural Distortion
God was interpreted through surrounding systems.

4. Emotional Decision
Fear entered and disguised itself as faith.

This is where the vow is born.

The Vow

"And Jephthah vowed a vow unto the LORD."
— Judges 11:30 KJV

He declared that if God granted victory, whatever first came out of his house would be offered as a burnt offering.

This was not obedience, it was negotiation.

Jephthah did not reject God—he attempted to secure Him. Instead of trusting the Lord's nature, he responded to internal pressure by creating a transaction God never required.

Fear had now taken the language of devotion.

The Outcome of Distorted Devotion

God granted Israel victory.

But when Jephthah returned, the first to greet him was his daughter.

"And behold, his daughter came out to meet him with timbrels and with dances."
— Judges 11:34 KJV

The moment exposes the cost of misunderstanding God. What was spoken in fear now demanded fulfillment in reality. The tragedy is not that Jephthah lacked sincerity, it is that his sincerity was guided by distortion. This reveals a sobering truth, Devotion without revelation can produce destruction.

The System Exposed

Judges 11 is not only about Jephthah—it is about how systems shape spiritual thinking. When people live long enough in environments that teach God must be persuaded, they begin to approach Him through performance rather than trust. Sacrifice becomes currency. Devotion becomes proof.

The relationship becomes a negotiation. This is not covenant—it is contamination deception straight from the kingdom of darkness.

Revelation Insight

Fear Produces Vows God Never Asked For

Jephthah's story reveals that fear, when rooted in wounded identity, will always seek control. And when control enters spiritual language, it disguises itself as devotion.

Fear says, "Secure the outcome."
Faith says, "Trust the One who already governs it."

Where fear is unhealed, people will make promises God never required in an attempt to gain what He already intended to give. But the gospel reveals a different foundation.

"Christ also hath once suffered for sins, the just for the unjust, that he might bring us to God."
— 1 Peter 3:18 KJV

The believer does not approach God to gain acceptance.
The believer approaches God from acceptance.

Where systems teach striving, Christ establishes rest.
Where fear produces vows, grace produces trust.

Modern Insight – Where Fear Still Speaks

The pattern revealed in Jephthah's life has not disappeared with time; it has only changed its language. What was once expressed through a spoken vow is now often formed internally, shaping decisions, expectations, and the way many approach God without ever being verbalized.

The same pressure that influenced Jephthah continues to operate wherever identity remains unsettled. When a person carries unhealed rejection or unresolved insecurity, their relationship with God can quietly shift from trust to effort. They may still speak the language of faith, yet internally they are attempting to secure outcomes rather than rest in what God has already established.

This is where fear becomes most deceptive. It rarely presents itself as fear. Instead, it appears as responsibility, urgency, or even devotion. A person may feel compelled to prove their commitment, to demonstrate their worth, or to ensure that nothing is left uncertain. What appears outwardly as dedication can, underneath, be driven by the same need that shaped Jephthah—the need to confirm identity through outcome.

Modern culture reinforces this pattern in silent but powerful ways. Systems built around performance, achievement, and visibility continually train individuals to associate value with results. Success becomes proof of worth, and failure becomes a threat to identity. Over time, this way of thinking can move from external influence to internal belief, shaping not only how a person views themselves, but how they believe God relates to them.

"But without faith it is impossible to please him..."
— Hebrews 11:6 KJV

In that environment, devotion can quietly become conditional. A person may not consciously attempt to bargain with God, yet their thinking reflects the same structure. They may feel that greater effort will produce greater favor, that increased sacrifice will secure greater outcomes, or that consistent performance will ensure continued acceptance. The language is different, but the logic remains the same.

What makes this pattern difficult to recognize is that it often coexists with genuine sincerity. Like Jephthah, a person can desire to honor God while still misunderstanding His nature.

They may act with intensity and commitment, yet their actions are shaped more by pressure than by trust. In this way, fear does not remove devotion—it redirects it.

"Not by works of righteousness which we have done, but according to his mercy he saved us..."
— Titus 3:5 KJV

This is why the distinction between faith and control is so critical. Faith rests in the character of God, while control attempts to manage His response. Faith moves from what God has already spoken, while control tries to secure what has not yet been seen. When fear is present, even spiritual actions can become attempts to stabilize uncertainty rather than expressions of trust.

The gospel confronts this distortion completely. It reveals that access to God is not achieved through performance, nor maintained through effort. The foundation has already been established through Christ. Relationship is not secured by what is promised to God, but by what God has already accomplished.

Where this truth is understood, the need to strive begins to lose its hold. Identity no longer depends on outcome, and devotion is no longer driven by pressure. Trust replaces negotiation, and obedience flows from assurance rather than fear. The question, then, is not whether a person would make a vow like Jephthah, but whether the same pattern exists in quieter forms. It appears anywhere there is an internal need to secure what God has already promised, or to prove what He has already declared. When fear is allowed to remain beneath the surface, it will eventually shape how God is perceived. And when God is perceived incorrectly, even sincere devotion can move in the wrong direction. But when truth reshapes perception, the cycle is broken.

The believer no longer approaches God trying to gain something that has already been given. Instead, they live from a place of established acceptance, where obedience is no longer a means of securing identity, but the result of it.

"Come unto me, all ye that labour and are heavy laden, and I will give you rest."
— Matthew 11:28 KJV

CHAPTER THIRTEEN

Esoteric Systems

Hidden Knowledge and Cultural Control

As Scripture reveals the development of civilizations and empires, it also exposes another pattern that appears repeatedly throughout human history: systems that organize knowledge in layers. In these systems certain teachings are presented openly to the general population, while deeper interpretations are reserved for select groups within the structure of power.

This arrangement is often described using the terms **exoteric** and **esoteric** knowledge.

Exoteric knowledge refers to teachings available to everyone within the culture. These include public rituals, moral instruction, religious celebrations, and traditions that reinforce social identity. Exoteric systems create a shared cultural framework that shapes how the population understands the world.

Esoteric knowledge, however, operates differently. It is knowledge interpreted or guarded by specialized groups—priests, scholars, or governing elites. These individuals claim authority to interpret symbols, signs, philosophical systems, or celestial movements that supposedly reveal deeper truths about reality and destiny.

Throughout ancient civilizations this layered structure allowed societies to maintain both unity and control.

The population participated in rituals and traditions, while those in positions of authority interpreted the deeper meanings behind those practices.

This pattern was particularly visible in the civilizations that shaped the ancient Near East.

Babylon and the Structure of Layered Knowledge

In Babylon, priestly classes studied celestial patterns and recorded the movements of stars and planets. These observations were interpreted as signs believed to influence human affairs and the destiny of nations. The priests who studied these patterns developed complex systems of interpretation that connected heavenly movements with earthly events.

While the general population participated in festivals and public worship rituals, the deeper interpretations of these signs were handled by those trained in specialized knowledge.

This created a structure in which society functioned on two levels.

The population practiced religion publicly through rituals and traditions. Meanwhile, those claiming deeper insight interpreted symbols, celestial events, and philosophical frameworks that supposedly revealed hidden meaning behind the visible world.

Such systems strengthened the authority of those who claimed to understand the deeper order of the universe. By controlling interpretation, they shaped how societies understood prosperity, destiny, and power.

Yet Scripture repeatedly warns that human systems built upon hidden knowledge can lead people away from dependence on God.

"Beware lest any man spoil you through philosophy and vain deceit, after the tradition of men, after the rudiments of the world, and not after Christ."
— ***Colossians 2:8 KJV***

The apostle Paul cautions believers that systems of philosophy and tradition can influence the mind in ways that obscure the truth revealed through Christ.

The Influence of Hidden Knowledge on Culture

When civilizations organize knowledge in layers, authority over interpretation becomes concentrated within institutions or elites. Over time this shapes the thinking of entire societies.

People begin to assume that understanding reality requires access to the interpreters of the system. Rituals are practiced without always understanding their meaning. Symbols become accepted as part of cultural identity, even when their origins are no longer clear.

This process creates psychological influence. Cultural systems slowly train individuals to depend on institutions for interpretation rather than seeking truth directly from God.

Such systems often promise enlightenment, power, or deeper understanding. Yet the more individuals rely on those systems, the further their thinking may drift from the simplicity of God's revealed word.

Scripture consistently contrasts this dependence on hidden knowledge with the openness of God's truth.

Jesus spoke openly about the message of the kingdom.

"I spake openly to the world... and in secret have I said nothing."
— John 18:20 KJV

The gospel is not built upon hidden teachings reserved for a select few. The truth of God's kingdom is proclaimed openly so that all who hear may respond.

Knowledge and the Human Desire for Control

The attraction of esoteric systems often lies in the promise of deeper understanding or influence. People naturally seek explanations for events in their lives and the world around them. Systems that claim to reveal hidden meaning can therefore appear compelling.

Yet the desire for hidden knowledge can also reflect a deeper human impulse—the desire for control.

If people believe certain knowledge grants influence over destiny, prosperity, or power, they may pursue that knowledge in hopes of securing advantage. Throughout history many systems have promised such control through symbolic interpretation, mystical understanding, or philosophical insight.

But the pursuit of knowledge apart from God often leads to confusion rather than wisdom.

"Professing themselves to be wise, they became fools."
— Romans 1:22 KJV

The Scriptures repeatedly remind believers that true wisdom begins not with hidden systems of interpretation but with reverence for God.

The Contrast Between Hidden Systems and Revealed Truth

The kingdom of God operates according to a fundamentally different principle. Instead of relying on secret knowledge held by elites, the gospel reveals truth openly through the word of God and the work of the Holy Spirit.

The apostle Paul described this revelation as something made known to believers through Christ.

"That the God of our Lord Jesus Christ... may give unto you the spirit of wisdom and revelation in the knowledge of him."
— Ephesians 1:17 KJV

In the kingdom of God understanding does not depend on belonging to a privileged group with access to hidden teachings. Instead, knowledge of God is revealed through Christ and made accessible to those who seek Him.

This distinction separates the systems of the world from the kingdom of God. Human systems often guard knowledge in order to maintain authority, while God reveals truth so that His people may walk in freedom, unentangled to darkness.

The Serpent Strategy Insight

The presence of hidden knowledge systems throughout history reflects a deeper pattern that Scripture reveals from the beginning.

The serpent's first strategy in the Garden of Eden involved altering how humanity perceived knowledge and authority.

"For God doth know that in the day ye eat thereof, then your eyes shall be opened."
— ***Genesis 3:5 KJV***

The serpent suggested that God had withheld knowledge that could elevate human understanding. By presenting the possibility of hidden insight, he shifted Eve's focus away from trusting God's command toward pursuing knowledge that appeared to offer advantage.

This moment reveals a pattern that continues throughout history.

The serpent often introduces the idea that truth exists beyond what God has revealed. Systems that promise deeper or hidden knowledge appeal to the human desire for understanding, influence, and status.

Once this desire takes hold, people may begin seeking knowledge through systems that claim special authority to interpret reality.

Yet Scripture reminds believers that the knowledge necessary for life and godliness has already been revealed.

"The secret things belong unto the LORD our God: but those things which are revealed belong unto us."
— ***Deuteronomy 29:29 KJV***

God's people are not called to pursue hidden systems of interpretation. They are called to walk in the truth that God has already revealed.

The serpent strategy attempts to redirect attention toward knowledge that appears exclusive or empowering. The gospel restores the focus of the believer toward trust in the word of God and the guidance of the Holy Spirit.

Where hidden systems promise enlightenment, Christ offers truth that leads to freedom.

"And ye shall know the truth, and the truth shall make you free."
— John 8:32 KJV

The freedom of the believer does not depend on access to secret knowledge but on a restored relationship with the One who is Himself the truth.

Renewing the Mind: Closing Access Points

After exposing how deception begins in the mind, grows into systems, and eventually shapes cultures and nations, the next question becomes unavoidable: how does a believer live free from those influences?

Scripture does not simply expose deception. It also reveals the path to transformation. That transformation begins in the mind.

"And be not conformed to this world: but be ye transformed by the renewing of your mind."
— Romans 12:2 KJV

The apostle Paul contrasts two processes occurring in every person's life. One is **conformation**, where the patterns of the world shape how a person thinks. The other is **transformation**, where the mind is renewed through the truth of God's Word.

The difference between these two processes determines whether a believer lives under the influence of worldly systems or walks in the freedom of Christ.

The Mind as the Battlefield

From the beginning of Scripture, the serpent's strategy has focused on the mind. In the Garden of Eden, the first temptation did not involve force or physical coercion. Instead, the serpent introduced a different way of thinking.

Eve's perception of God's command was altered before the act of disobedience occurred.

This pattern continues throughout Scripture. Deception rarely begins with outward behavior. It begins with thoughts, perceptions, and interpretations.

The apostle Paul described this battle in deep personal terms.

"For the good that I would I do not: but the evil which I would not, that I do."
— Romans 7:19 KJV

Paul's words reveal the tension between the renewed spirit and the lingering patterns of the flesh. Even after encountering the truth, believers may find themselves wrestling with old ways of thinking shaped by past influences. The enemy studies these patterns carefully. Emotional wounds, fears, and habits formed before conversion can become points of pressure where the mind struggles to align with the truth.

Access Points of Influence

The systems described in earlier chapters—Babylon, cultural narratives, hidden knowledge structures, and national influence attempt to shape human thinking over long periods of time. These influences do not disappear instantly when a person comes to faith.

They leave **mental patterns**.

These patterns can become what might be called **access points**. They are places where the mind remains vulnerable to suggestions that contradict God's truth.

Access points may develop through several avenues:

1. **Cultural Conditioning**
   Beliefs absorbed through education, traditions, and social expectations.
2. **Emotional Wounds**
   Experiences of rejection, fear, or insecurity that influence how a person interprets circumstances.
3. **Past Habits of Thinking**
   Long-standing patterns formed before a person understood the truth of the gospel.
4. **False Narratives**
   Ideas about identity, success, or power that originate in worldly systems rather than Scripture.

These influences shape how individuals perceive reality unless they are brought under the authority of God's Word.

The Process of Renewal

Renewing the mind is not a single event but a continuing process. As believers encounter the truth of Scripture, the Holy Spirit begins reshaping their understanding.

This renewal occurs through several key practices.

1. Immersion in the Word of God

God's Word provides the standard by which all thoughts and ideas must be measured.

"Sanctify them through thy truth: thy word is truth."
— John 17:17 KJV

As the believer studies Scripture, old patterns of thinking are confronted and replaced with the truth.

2. Discernment of Thoughts

Believers are called to examine the ideas that enter their minds.

"Casting down imaginations, and every high thing that exalteth itself against the knowledge of God."
— 2 Corinthians 10:5 KJV

This passage describes an active process of rejecting thoughts that contradict God's revealed truth.

3. Dependence on the Holy Spirit

Renewal ultimately occurs through the work of the Holy Spirit, who guides believers into understanding.

"Howbeit when he, the Spirit of truth, is come, he will guide you into all truth."
— John 16:13 KJV

The Spirit illuminates Scripture and reveals areas where thinking must change.

Transformation of Identity

As the mind is renewed, the believer begins to see identity differently.

Worldly systems define people through achievement, status, cultural affiliation, or personal success. These systems constantly reinforce the idea that value must be earned or demonstrated. The gospel offers a different foundation.

"If any man be in Christ, he is a new creature."
— 2 Corinthians 5:17 KJV

Identity is no longer determined by past patterns or cultural narratives. It is rooted in the relationship established through Christ. This transformation gradually reshapes the way believers respond to challenges, authority, and cultural pressures.

Guarding the Mind

Renewal must also be protected. The mind remains the place where influences compete for attention.

Scripture encourages believers to guard what enters their thoughts.

"Keep thy heart with all diligence, for out of it are the issues of life."
— Proverbs 4:23 KJV

Yet guarding the mind does not mean withdrawing from the world but exercising discernment regarding ideas, teachings, and influences through the lens of scripture. As believers we are to test everything against God's word, we are to hold fast to what is true and discard what is not. This is an ongoing practice we must do daily picking up our cross and following Christ. We must filter ideas that keep us anchored in truth. We are to ask the Holy Spirit to reveal any influences we might miss, ensuring that our minds aren't just protected but continually transformed, reflecting Christ's perspective more. In doing this it cultivates the mind to fully align with God's will for our life.

Living with a Renewed Mind

When the mind is renewed, the believer becomes less vulnerable to the pressures of systems described in earlier chapters.

Cultural narratives lose their power to define identity. Fear no longer dictates decisions. Hidden systems that claim authority over truth lose their influence.

Instead, the believer begins to walk in the freedom that comes from alignment with God's Word.

Renewal does not remove the believer from the world but enables them to live within it without being shaped by its systems.

The Serpent Strategy Insight

The serpent's strategy throughout history has relied on shaping human perception. If the mind can be persuaded to accept distorted narratives about God, identity, or authority, behavior will eventually follow. This is why the battle for the mind remains central.

The enemy attempts to keep old patterns of thinking alive so that believers interpret circumstances through fear, pride, or insecurity rather than through faith.

Renewing the mind closes these access points. As the truth of Scripture reshapes understanding, the influence of deceptive systems begins to weaken.

What once appeared convincing is recognized as delusion.

The believer learns to evaluate every thought against the revealed truth of God's Word.

Christ: The Source of True Renewal

The renewal of the mind ultimately depends on the work of Christ. Through His death and resurrection believers receive not only forgiveness but also the power for transformation.

"*Let this mind be in you, which was also in Christ Jesus.*"
— ***Philippians 2:5 KJV***

The mind of Christ reflects humility, obedience, and complete trust in the Father. As believers grow in their relationship with Him, their thinking gradually aligns with His character. The process of renewal therefore leads not simply to better behavior but to deeper conformity to Christ Himself. Through Him the mind is renewed, access points are closed, and the believer begins to walk in the freedom of the kingdom of God.

CHAPTER FOURTEEN

False Refuge: Returning to Egypt

After the mind begins to renew and truth becomes clearer, another danger often appears. Exposure alone does not guarantee transformation. Even when people recognize deception, the pull of familiar systems can remain strong. Scripture repeatedly reveals that one of the most persistent temptations facing God's people is the desire to return to what God has already delivered them from.

Throughout the biblical narrative Egypt becomes a symbol of this temptation. It represents more than a physical location. Egypt represents a system built on power, control, and dependence on human authority rather than trust in God.

When the Lord delivered Israel from Egypt, He was not only freeing them from slavery. He was separating them from a system that shaped their identity, labor, economy, and daily existence. Pharaoh governed every aspect of life. Though oppressive, the system provided structure and predictability.

Once the people left Egypt, they entered the wilderness where that structure no longer existed. Instead of relying on a visible system, they were learning to depend directly on God.

"And the children of Israel said unto them, Would to God we had died by the hand of the LORD in the land of Egypt."
— Exodus 16:3 KJV

This statement reveals an important psychological reality. Even though Egypt had enslaved them, the memory of the system began to appear safer than the uncertainty of trusting God.

The wilderness exposed a struggle within the mind. Freedom required a new way of thinking, but the old system remained familiar.

The Psychology of Remembering Egypt

Human memory does not always preserve the past accurately. When fear or uncertainty arises, the mind often reshapes memory in ways that make the past appear more stable than it truly was.

The Israelites began remembering Egypt not as a place of bondage but as a place where food, structure, and predictability existed.

"Wherefore have ye made us to come up out of Egypt?"
— Numbers 21:5 KJV

The hardship of the wilderness caused the people to reinterpret their past. What once represented oppression began to appear like security.

This pattern reveals the psychological pull of familiar systems. When individuals face uncertainty, the mind may prefer a system it understands—even if that system once produced suffering.

Freedom requires learning to trust God in unfamiliar territory, and that process can feel unstable until faith matures.

When Fear Overrides Obedience

The pattern of returning to Egypt appears again centuries later during one of the most tragic moments in Israel's history. After Jerusalem fell to Babylon, a small remnant of people remained in the land. Fear spread throughout the community, and the people sought guidance from the prophet Jeremiah.

They approached him with what sounded like sincere humility.

"Pray for us unto the LORD thy God... that the LORD thy God may shew us the way wherein we may walk."
— Jeremiah 42:2–3 KJV

They promised to obey whatever the Lord revealed.

After seeking God in prayer, Jeremiah delivered the answer. The Lord instructed the people not to flee to Egypt. If they remained in the land and trusted Him, He would protect them.

But the response revealed the deeper struggle in their hearts.

"Thou speakest falsely: the LORD our God hath not sent thee."
— Jeremiah 43:2 KJV

Fear overpowered their willingness to trust God. Instead of obeying the instruction they had asked for, they accused the prophet of deception and led the people into Egypt anyway.

This moment exposes the psychology of false refuge. The people believed Egypt offered greater security than obedience to God.

The Prosperity Illusion

Once the people settled in Egypt, their reasoning became even clearer. They explained why they believed life had been better under earlier systems of worship.

"For then had we plenty of victuals, and were well, and saw no evil."
— Jeremiah 44:17 KJV

Their memory of the past had been reshaped by the desire for prosperity and stability. They concluded that their previous religious practices had produced better results.

This reveals the deeper issue behind false refuge. The people were not simply seeking physical safety. They were seeking the prosperity and stability they believed certain systems could provide.

Instead of trusting the Lord, they trusted a familiar structure that appeared to guarantee security.

Looking Back Instead of Forward

The temptation to return to Egypt also appears in other moments throughout Scripture. One of the most striking examples occurs in the story of Lot's wife.

When God delivered Lot and his family from the destruction of Sodom, they were given a clear command.

"Look not behind thee."
— Genesis 19:17 KJV

Yet Lot's wife looked back.

"But his wife looked back from behind him, and she became a pillar of salt."
— Genesis 19:26 KJV

Her glance backward symbolized more than curiosity. It revealed attachment to the life she was leaving behind.

This pattern appears repeatedly in the human heart. Deliverance requires leaving something behind, but attachment to the past can weaken the resolve to move forward.

False Refuge in the Mind

Returning to Egypt is not only a physical act. It can occur within the mind. Believers who have been delivered from destructive patterns may still feel the pull of those patterns when facing pressure, uncertainty, or fear. Familiar habits of thinking may attempt to reassert themselves. This is why the renewal of the mind described in the previous chapter is essential.

"Stand fast therefore in the liberty wherewith Christ hath made us free."
— Galatians 5:1 KJV

Freedom must be guarded. Without renewed thinking, the mind may reinterpret past bondage as comfort and attempt to return to the systems God has already broken.

The Serpent Strategy Insight

The serpent's strategy often relies on reshaping the way people remember and interpret the past. If the mind can be persuaded that former systems offered security or prosperity, returning to those systems can appear reasonable.

Fear becomes the doorway for this deception. When the future seems uncertain, the mind may begin romanticizing the structures that once defined life.

The enemy does not need to rebuild the old system if the mind willingly returns to it.

By altering memory and perception, the serpent creates the illusion that bondage was safety and freedom is instability.

But Scripture repeatedly reminds God's people that the systems of the world cannot provide true refuge.

Christ: The True Refuge

The deliverance from Egypt ultimately points forward to a greater deliverance through Christ. Just as God rescued Israel from Pharaoh, Jesus rescues humanity from sin and from the systems that enslave the human heart.

The gospel does more than remove external oppression. It transforms the mind and establishes a new identity rooted in Christ.

"If the Son therefore shall make you free, ye shall be free indeed."
— John 8:36 KJV

The freedom Christ provides replaces the need for false refuge. The believer no longer depends on systems of power, wealth, or control for security.

Instead, refuge is found in the kingdom of God.

Where Egypt offered temporary stability through human authority, Christ offers lasting freedom through His truth.

Those who walk in that freedom no longer look backward toward Egypt. They move forward in faith toward the kingdom that cannot be shaken.

CHAPTER FIFTEEN

The End of the Old System: Death Before Alignment

The progression of revelation always leads to a necessary confrontation, what has been revealed must eventually be removed. Exposure alone is not transformation. Understanding without separation leaves systems intact. What has been seen must now be severed.

Throughout the previous chapters, patterns have been uncovered. Systems have been exposed. The strategies that shape thought, identity, and behavior have been brought into view. Yet recognition alone does not dismantle what has been built over time. There must be an end to what no longer aligns GOD will not be mocked…

Scripture does not present transformation as modification. It presents it as death.

This is where the message of Hebrews becomes essential.

The End of Repetition

The system that existed before Christ was built on a duplication of what was taught by a generation before. Sacrifices were offered continually, not because they perfected the worshipper, but because they revealed the inability of the system to complete what it began.

"For the law having a shadow of good things to come... can never with those sacrifices which they offered year by year continually make the comers thereunto perfect."
— Hebrews 10:1 KJV

The patterns they picked up exposed their shortcomings.

What could not be completed had to be repeated. What had to be repeated could never fully resolve the condition of the heart. The system addressed behavior temporarily, but it did not transform your nature permanently.

This is the pattern of every incomplete system. It manages symptoms but never changes identity.

Hebrews reveals that Christ did not enter into that cycle—He ended it.

"But this man, after he had offered one sacrifice for sins for ever, sat down on the right hand of God."
— Hebrews 10:12 (KJV)

The posture of Christ—*seated*—is revelation.

The work is not ongoing. It is finished.

A Finished Work Cannot Be Supplemented

Where something is complete, it cannot be added to without being misunderstood.

The system of sacrifice has ended, yet many continue to live as if something still needs to be secured. This is where psychological patterns collide with spiritual truth. When the mind has been trained by systems of performance, it struggles to accept what has already been completed. The result is gentle but significant.

People begin to live as though they must maintain what Christ has already finished. Effort replaces trust. Repetition then replaces rest. Your devotion becomes driven by pressure rather than alignment with the word. But Hebrews removes that possibility.

"For by one offering he hath perfected for ever them that are sanctified."
— Hebrews 10:14 KJV

This statement does not describe a process—it declares a position.

What Christ finished externally must now be agreed with internally.

The Necessary Response— Death to the Old Pattern

If Christ has ended the system, then what remains is not improvement—it is separation.

This is where Colossians speak directly to you as a believer:

"Mortify therefore your members which are upon the earth..."
— Colossians 3:5 KJV

The instruction is not to manage, negotiate, or slowly reduce, it is to put to death pick up your cross and follow Jesus. This is a choice all believers must choose.

This is not physical, it is structural.

It is the ending of patterns that were formed under a different system. It is the refusal to allow old frameworks of thinking, reacting, and striving to remain active where truth has already replaced them. Mortification is not punishment; it is alignment with truth. What no longer belongs must no longer live.

It must be crucified with Christ.

The Psychology of Letting Go

The difficulty of this command is not in understanding it—it is in releasing what has become familiar. Things done out of habit or from prior generations. Systems, once internalized, do not feel external. They feel like identity.

This is why the instruction is direct.

Because what feels natural may not be original.
What feels right may have been learned.
What feels necessary may no longer be true.

To mortify means put to(death)is to recognize that what once governed you no longer has over you, we must die daily that we walk in authority.

This includes:

the need to prove
the need to secure
the need to perform
the need to control outcomes

These are not simply behaviors—they are responses formed under a system that Christ has already ended.

The Shift from Effort to Alignment

The believer is not called to recreate what Christ has done. They are called to align with it.

This is the shift:

From striving → to standing
From repetition → to rest
From performance → to position

Hebrews establishes the foundation.
Colossians enforces the response.

Together, they reveal that transformation is not achieved by adding something new, it is completed by removing what no longer belongs.

Revelation Insight

Death Is Not Loss – It Is Release

The ending of a system often feels like loss because it requires the surrender of what has been familiar. Yet what is being removed was never sustaining—it was maintained. Christ did not come to improve the old system—He came to end it. Where the old, required repetition, the new establishes completion. Where the old, required effort, the new establishes access. Where the old, maintained distance, the new creates relationship.

The instruction to "**mortify**" is not a call to struggle—it is a call to agreement.

To agree that what has already been finished no longer needs to be managed.
To agree that what Christ has removed no longer needs to be carried.
To agree that what once defined you no longer has authority over you.

Transition

Before Christ can be understood as the Author and Finisher of your faith, the systems that once authored your thinking must be brought to an end. Only then can what He finishes becomes what you live from. If the former structure remains in place, it continues to influence how truth is received, filtering what has already been formed.

This is why transformation requires, more than acknowledgement, it requires a separation from what has been controlling your response. What Christ finished does not adjust your previous patterns, it replaces them. When the former influence is no longer guiding thought, what He established becomes the foundation, and life begins to flow from what has been completed rather than controlled.

CHAPTER SIXTEEN

Christ: The Author and Finisher

Throughout Scripture the rise and fall of civilizations reveal a recurring pattern. Nations build systems of power, influence, and control that appear stable for a time, yet eventually every human structure begins to crumble.

Empires that once dominated the world fade into history, and systems that promised prosperity and security prove unable to sustain themselves.

The Bible does not simply record these historical changes. It reveals the spiritual reality behind them. Human systems rise through ambition, power, and the desire to control resources, people, and knowledge. Yet Scripture repeatedly reminds us that these systems operate within limits established by God.

From the earliest chapters of Genesis, the serpent introduced a competing vision for humanity—one that encouraged independence from God and reliance on human understanding. This deception influenced individuals first, but over time it shaped entire civilizations.

The result was the development of cultural, political, and religious systems that appeared strong but ultimately drew people away from dependence on the Creator.

Yet the story of Scripture does not end with the triumph of these systems. Instead, the Bible consistently points toward a kingdom established by God Himself.

At the center of that kingdom stands Jesus Christ.

The Pattern of Deliverance in Scripture

One of the clearest demonstrations of God's power over oppressive systems appears in the deliverance of Israel from Egypt. Pharaoh's empire represented a structure of authority that controlled labor, resources, and identity. For generations the Israelites lived under this system, believing its power was unbreakable.

Yet through a series of divine interventions, God dismantled Pharaoh's authority. The plagues exposed the weakness of Egypt's gods, and the crossing of the Red Sea revealed that the Lord alone held ultimate power.

When the Israelites saw their deliverance, they responded with worship.

"Then sang Moses and the children of Israel this song unto the LORD."
— Exodus 15:1 KJV

The Song of Moses celebrated the defeat of a system that had once appeared invincible. Pharaoh's army lay destroyed, and the people recognized that their freedom had come entirely from the Lord.

But Egypt was not the final oppressive system humanity would encounter. As history unfolded, new empires emerged—Babylon, Persia, Greece, and Rome. Each of these civilizations developed powerful structures that shaped the political, cultural, and economic landscape of their time.

Despite their strength, Scripture consistently reminds us that no human empire can endure forever.

"And in the days of these kings shall the God of heaven set up a kingdom, which shall never be destroyed."
— Daniel 2:44 KJV

This prophecy revealed that God would establish a kingdom fundamentally different from the systems that had dominated human history.

The Kingdom Revealed Through Christ

Jesus Christ entered the world as the fulfillment of this promise. Unlike earthly rulers, He did not establish authority through military conquest or political alliances. Instead, His ministry revealed a kingdom built upon truth, humility, and obedience to God.

Jesus announced the arrival of this kingdom with a simple yet powerful message.

"The time is fulfilled, and the kingdom of God is at hand: repent ye, and believe the gospel."
— Mark 1:15 KJV

The kingdom Jesus proclaimed did not depend on the structures of human government. Its authority flowed directly from God, and its citizens were defined not by nationality or social status but by their relationship with Him.

Where the systems of the world pursue power through dominance, the kingdom of God advances through transformation of the human heart.

The Transformation of the Mind

Earlier chapters of this book have examined the psychological dimension of spiritual warfare. Systems influence societies, but the most decisive battlefield remains the human mind.

If perception can be altered, behavior eventually follows. The serpent's original strategy in Eden relied on reshaping how humanity interpreted God's command.

Christ reverses that distortion by restoring the mind to truth.

Through His death and resurrection believers receive not only forgiveness but also the possibility of transformation.

"Therefore if any man be in Christ, he is a new creature."
— 2 Corinthians 5:17 KJV

This transformation reshapes identity. Instead of defining themselves through the systems of culture, believers discover their identity in Christ. As the mind is renewed through Scripture and the guidance of the Holy Spirit, the influence of deceptive narratives begins to weaken.

The systems that once shaped thinking lose their authority.

The Fall of World Systems

The final chapters of Scripture reveal that the systems dominating human history will ultimately collapse. The book of Revelation describes the fall of Babylon, symbolizing the culmination of human civilization built on pride, wealth, and exploitation.

"Babylon the great is fallen, is fallen."
— Revelation 18:2 KJV

This declaration signals the end of the world system that has drawn humanity away from God. The structures that once promised prosperity and power are exposed as temporary and unstable.

At that moment the authority of Christ becomes fully visible.

"The kingdoms of this world are become the kingdoms of our Lord, and of his Christ."
— Revelation 11:15 KJV

The kingdom of God replaces every system that once claimed authority over the nations.

The Song of Moses and the Song of the Lamb

At the culmination of this victory, Scripture presents a remarkable scene. The people of God once again lift their voices in worship.

"And they sing the song of Moses the servant of God, and the song of the Lamb."
— Revelation 15:3 KJV

This moment connects the deliverance of Israel from Egypt with the final triumph of Christ over every oppressive system.

The Song of Moses celebrated freedom from Pharaoh's empire.
The Song of the Lamb celebrates the defeat of every system that has opposed God throughout history.

Both songs proclaim the same truth: the Lord alone delivers His people.

The pattern revealed in Exodus reaches its ultimate fulfillment in Christ.

The Serpent Strategy Insight

Throughout history the serpent's strategy has relied on shaping human perception. By influencing the mind, systems of power attempt to redirect trust away from God and toward human authority.

These systems promise prosperity, identity, and security. Yet their foundations remain unstable because they depend on human ambition rather than divine truth.

The serpent encourages humanity to believe that power and stability can be achieved through control of systems—economic, political, or cultural.

Christ exposes this deception.

His kingdom does not arise from manipulation or domination. Instead, it is built upon obedience to the Father and the transformation of the human heart.

Where the serpent promotes independence from God, Christ restores relationship with Him.
Where worldly systems promise security through power, Christ reveals peace through trust in God.

A Call to Discernment

The exposure of these systems carries an important responsibility for believers. Understanding the patterns of deception described throughout Scripture should lead to greater discernment.

Believers are called to examine the ideas, structures, and narratives that shape the world around them.

"Prove all things; hold fast that which is good."
— 1 Thessalonians 5:21 KJV

Discernment allows the believer to live within society without becoming captive of the systems that influence it.

Rather than placing their hope in human institutions, believers anchor their faith in the kingdom of God.

The Author and Finisher

The journey of faith ultimately begins and ends with Christ.

"Looking unto Jesus the author and finisher of our faith."
— Hebrews 12:2 KJV

He is the author who initiates redemption and the finisher who brings God's plan to completion. Every chapter of Scripture points toward Him, and every system that has attempted to replace God ultimately collapses before His authority.

Through Christ believers find the freedom that no human structure can provide. Their identity is no longer determined by the systems of the world but by their relationship with the King whose kingdom will never pass away. And unlike the empires of history, the kingdom of Christ will stand forever.

The Foundation That Remains

After examining the systems of deception and the battle for the mind, the focus returns to the only foundation that remains unshaken, the works, truth, and covenant of God.

The foundation that stands firm after the complexities of deception and the struggle in the mind is none other than Christ Himself. He is the cornerstone upon which everything true and lasting is built. As Paul wrote,

"For other foundation can no man lay than that is laid, which is Jesus Christ"

—1 Corinthians 3:11 KJV

It is on Him that we are built up as a spiritual house,

"And are built upon the foundation of the apostles and prophets, Jesus Christ himself being the chief cornerstone"

—Ephesians 2:20 KJV

When all else is shaken, the believer stands firm on Christ. As Jesus Himself declared,

"Upon this rock I will build my church; and the gates of hell shall not prevail against it"

—Matthew 16:18 KJV

Thus, returning to Him, the living cornerstone, ensures that truth and covenant remain unshaken. As Peter affirmed,

"Behold, I lay in Zion a chief corner stone, elect, precious, and he that believeth on him shall not be confounded"

—1 Peter 2:6 KJV

Psalm 111 KJV

Praise ye the LORD. I will praise the LORD with my whole heart, in the assembly of the upright, and in the congregation.

The works of the LORD are great, sought out of all them that have pleasure therein.

His work is honourable and glorious: and his righteousness endureth for ever.

He hath made his wonderful works to be remembered: the LORD is gracious and full of compassion.

He hath given meat unto them that fear him: he will ever be mindful of his covenant.

He hath shewed his people the power of his works, that he may give them the heritage of the heathen.

The works of his hands are verity and judgment; all his commandments are sure.

They stand fast for ever and ever, and are done in truth and uprightness.

He sent redemption unto his people: he hath commanded his covenant for ever: holy and reverend is his name.

The fear of the LORD is the beginning of wisdom: a good understanding have all they that do his commandments: his praise endureth forever.

The fear of the LORD is the beginning of wisdom.
Where truth is established, deception loses its power.

Discernment Calendar

The appointed times given in Leviticus 23 were never an end in themselves. They were shadows—divinely structured moments pointing forward to Christ. Each feast revealed a part of God's redemptive plan, from the sacrifice of the Lamb to the dwelling of God with His people.

Yet these were not given for perpetual observance apart from understanding. They were fulfilled.

"Which are a shadow of things to come; but the body is of Christ."
— Colossians 2:17 KJV

Christ is our Passover.
He is our atonement.
He is the fulfillment of what the feasts revealed.

The purpose, therefore, is not to return to the shadow, but to recognize the substance and not just ritual, but the revelation. Not repetition, but the fulfillment. Christ is not a symbol of the feasts—He is the ultimate fulfillment of it. He is risen….

"For even Christ our passover is sacrificed for us."
— 1 Corinthians 5:7 KJV

He is not only the Lamb, but the atonement once required year after year.

"And he is the propitiation for our sins…"
— 1 John 2:2 KJV

What was once repeated has now been fulfilled.

"By one offering he hath perfected for ever them that are sanctified."
— Hebrews 10:14 KJV

Systems of Time: How Worship Was Redirected

Time, as established by God, was never intended to be neutral. It was created as a structure through which His order, authority, and redemptive plan would be revealed. From the beginning, time was tied to alignment for his purpose.

"Let them be for signs, and for seasons…"
— Genesis 1:14 KJV

The word used for seasons—*moedim*—does not describe general cycles. It refers to appointed encounters, fixed moments where heaven and earth intersect according to God's design. Time, therefore, was not simply measured—it was governed.

This is why the alteration of time is not a minor shift. It is a strategic one.

"He shall think to change times and laws…"
— Daniel 7:25 KJV

This reveals not only an action, but an intention. If time defines when people gather, celebrate, and remember, then altering time reshapes what you value, what you honor, and ultimately what you align with.

Worship is not removed; it is redirected to distract and deceive your thinking. **This is the real strategy**.

God's appointed times, outlined in **Leviticus 23**, form a complete structure centered on Christ—redemption through the Lamb, separation from sin, resurrection, transformation through the Holy Spirit, and the dwelling of God with His people. These were not given as optional observances, but as a rhythm of alignment, ensuring that remembrance was not left to the emotion, but anchored in obedience.

When this structure is replaced, something deeper happens than the introduction of new traditions. The framework that once revealed truth begins to be overlaid with systems rooted in earlier forms of worship—systems that trained people to understand life, power, and identity apart from God.

What appears today as widely accepted cultural observances—such as the winter-Christmas celebration commonly associated with the birth of Christ, the spring-easter observance tied to resurrection, or the fall-halloween and thanksgiving traditions centered around death and fear and thanks to their pagan gods often carries the imprint of those earlier systems.

December 25, now recognized globally as the celebration of Christ's birth, it was not derived from Scripture. What is now called **Christmas** developed within an already existing **Roman structure—aligned with festivals such as Saturnalia and the observance of Sol Invictus, the "unconquered sun."** These were not merely seasonal gatherings, but systems that honored *created* *light*, excess, and *cyclical identity*. When the language of Christ was placed into that structure,

The winter celebration now recognized as Christmas follows a similar pattern of transformation. What is widely understood as the celebration of Christ's birth did not originate from Scripture but was placed within an already existing seasonal framework.

In the Roman world, late December was marked by festivals such as **Saturnalia** and the observance of **Sol Invictus**—the **"unconquered sun**." These celebrations were centered on themes of light emerging from darkness, renewal of the sun's strength, and communal expressions of excess, gift-giving, and reversal of social order.

This was not simply a seasonal celebration.
It was a system.

Light was honored—not as the Creator, but as the creation.
Renewal was understood but not through redemption, through cosmic cycles.

When the birth of Christ began to be associated with this time of year, the structure itself remained. The language changed, but the framework already carried meaning. What was once celebrated the created light was now overlaid with the declaration of *Christ as the Light of the world.*

This marks the point of redirection.

In its redeemed expression, the focus becomes clear:

"God is light, and in him is no darkness at all."
— 1 John 1:5 KJV

Christ is not a seasonal symbol of light. He is the source of it the light, he is the Light of the World, yet darkness still remains.

The modern expression of Christmas often reflects both structures—honoring Christ while simultaneously reinforcing patterns of materialism, emotional expectation, and identity shaped by tradition. What was intended to point to divine truth is often experienced through cultural rituals disguised as traditions and heritage.

This reveals the same principle.

A system may be redirected,
but if its foundation is not fully restructured,
its original patterns can continue to shape perception to manipulate the mind.

The spring observance known as ***Easter*** presents another example of this layered structure. While it is associated with the resurrection of Christ, its framework does not originate from the biblical timing established in Passover.

In Scripture, the death and resurrection of Christ are directly tied to ***Passover***—the moment of deliverance through the Lamb. This timing is not symbolic alone; it is precise.

"Christ our Passover is sacrificed for us."
— 1 Corinthians 5:7 KJV

Yet the observance now known as Easter another structure was formed from Eostre known as a goddess honored by the English developed within a different framework, historically connected to **fertility systems** that marked the renewal of life through nature. These systems emphasized reproduction, seasonal cycles, and the continuation of life through the earth.

This distinction is critical The Resurrection, as revealed in Scripture, is not cyclical.
It is decisive. It is not the continuation of life. It is victory over death.
He is the Way The Truth and The Life….

The symbols that remain eggs and rabbits—reflect the original framework of fertility and reproduction. Life is presented as something that repeats, rather than something that has been transformed.

When the Resurrection of Christ is remembered within that structure, the meaning can quietly shift. What is meant to reveal redemption can be interpreted through rituals never uprooted.

In its redeemed expression, however, the truth remains unchanged.

Christ did not rise as part of a cycle.
He rose to end one.

"Now is Christ risen from the dead, and become the firstfruits..."
— 1 Corinthians 15:20 KJV

Modern systems often blend both meanings, acknowledging resurrection while engaging symbols that communicate a different foundation. What was intended to reveal victory can be experienced as tradition and ritual practices. Some would say it's just fun. You choose who and what you will serve....

In the fall, what is now recognized as **Halloween** reveals a different dimension of the same pattern. Unlike other observances that developed around a central named **deity,** this system was rooted in something broader and more immersive—a worldview centered on the spirit realm itself.

Its pagan origin traces back to the ancient **Celtic festival of Samhain**, observed at the transition between harvest and winter. This period was believed to mark a thinning between the living and dead what was understood as the Otherworld, a realm inhabited by spirits, the dead, and unseen forces. They honored a few pagan gods such as Pomona goddess of fruits and orchards.

Within this system, spiritual activity was expected they interacted with spirits of the dead.

Fires were lit, offerings were made, and disguises were worn to hide themselves from other ghosts, as participation in a belief that the unseen could move freely among the living. Practices of divination were common, as people sought knowledge, protection, or favor from forces beyond the natural.

Though not centered on one deity alone, this system operated within the domain of figures such as the **Dagda—associated with life, death, and the underworld**—and the **Morrigan, linked to fate, death, and spiritual conflict.** These were not always the object of direct worship within the festival itself, but they represented the governing powers of the spiritual realm they were tied to, the hidden demonic parts in the background.

This is what defined the structure. It was not simply about honoring a god. It was about accessing a realm of demonic spirits that they worshiped they thought would protect them.

Over time, this framework was not removed, but reinterpreted. What was once tied to ritual interaction with spirits was gradually reshaped into a cultural celebration. The language softened, and the practices adapted to the way of life, but the themes remained. It became a part of the culture like today.

The Darkness became costumes. Fear became entertainment. Death became familiar.

Yet Scripture presents a clear contrast:

"Have no fellowship with the unfruitful works of darkness…"
— Ephesians 5:11 KJV

What was once approached with caution is now approached casually with no fear of GOD.

And through these traditions, what once signified danger becomes normalized and excepted today.

This reveals the same underlying principle seen throughout these systems. What begins in the spiritual realm of influence does not remain hidden, it travels, it settles and it takes form within culture until its origin is forgotten, yet its influence continues, directing and shaping thoughts and characters of individual's lives, establishing patterns without anyone tracing it back to its source. Nowadays it is called heritage and traditions that only a few may question. Jesus also said a narrow road only a few may enter.

The issue is not merely the presence of the symbols. It is the formation that occurs through participation. Often times what is repeated most people become accustomed and attached, and what becomes a routine is rarely questioned.

Even celebrations centered around love, such as **Valentine's Day**, reflect a similar shift. What originated through systems tied to a roman god of love or cupid or Greek eros known for desire and affection, emotional expression now shapes modern understanding of love. Love becomes defined by feeling rather than gods covenant, by validation rather than sacrifice. In this way, what God established as a reflection of His nature becomes reinterpreted through human emotion. In ancient Rome, the period in mid-February was marked by **Lupercalia festival** centered on purification, fertility, and reproduction. Rituals included animal sacrifice and practices believed to promote fruitfulness, particularly among women. Relationships during this time were not defined by commitment, but by pairing and physical union, reflecting a system that understood life through biological continuation rather than covenantal design.

This framework trained people to associate love with desire, reproduction, and seasonal cycles.

Over time, as Christianity spread, the structure of the festivals was not entirely removed, but reinterpreted. The name of **Valentine**—associated with early Christian accounts of a man who honored marriage and commitment—became attached to the same timeframe. What had once centered on ritual and fertility began to shift toward the idea of love expressed through devotion.

This marks a transition.

Not from existence to absence, but from one meaning to another.

What was once rooted in ritual was given the opportunity to be redefined through interpreting as truth. Unfortunately, it remains today.

In its redeemed expression, love reflects the nature of God—covenant, sacrifice, and commitment.

"God is love."
— 1 John 4:8 KJV

"Husbands, love your wives, even as Christ also loved the church..."
— Ephesians 5:25 KJV

The modern expression of Valentine's Day often reflects both influences—celebration mixed with expectation, affection shaped by feeling, and identity tied to emotional validation. What was introduced as a redirection toward commitment now operates within a culture that often defines love apart from God's covenant.

This reveals a deeper principle.

A system may be renamed…
It may be rebranded...
It may even be redirected…

But unless its foundation is fully aligned with truth of God's word its elements of its original structure can continue to shape how it is understood.

The question, then, is not simply whether something has been redeemed.

It is whether what remains continues to form the heart in alignment with God's definition—or in agreement with what the serpent wants from you. **Your Worship.**

The beginning of the year itself reflects this alteration. Scripture establishes time beginning in redemption:

"This month shall be unto you the beginning of months..."
— Exodus 12:2 KJV

Yet what is now observed as the **New Year** follows a different structure, rooted in Roman timekeeping and associated with transitions rather than transformation. The result is a cycle where people reset intentions without addressing nature, moving forward in time while remaining unchanged internally. These are not isolated examples, but visible expressions of a broader pattern—where systems once rooted in specific forms of worship are adapted, renamed, and integrated until their origins are no longer questioned.

What these systems originally trained has not disappeared. It has simply been absorbed into modern life.

Fertility systems trained people to see life as cyclical.
Solar systems trained people to look to created light as sustaining power.
Death-centered systems trained people to engage fear as a force.
Emotional systems trained people to define truth by feeling rather than by God.

Over time, these patterns no longer appear spiritual—they appear normal. This is how systems remain effective without being recognized. People celebrate without understanding the origin.
They participate without examining the structure.
They inherit traditions without questioning the formation.

And through repetition, these patterns shape the perception.

"Beware lest any man spoil you through philosophy and vain deceit, after the tradition of men..."
— Colossians 2:8 KJV

The concern is not tradition itself, but tradition that replaces truth as the framework through which life is to be lived through Christ Jesus. The deeper issue is not the celebration, it is the formation and what spirit is operating behind its darkness or light. These things must be discerned through the Holy Spirit.

The serpent's strategy has never required the removal of truth. It requires the restructuring of the systems that reveal it.

If time is altered, remembrance is altered.
If remembrance is altered, meaning is altered.
If meaning is altered, alignment is altered.

And once alignment is altered, the shift often goes unnoticed. Scripture reminds us that this is not a natural conflict, but a spiritual one.

"For we wrestle not against flesh and blood, but against principalities, against powers, against the rulers of the darkness of this world, against spiritual wickedness in high places."
— Ephesians 6:12 KJV

We are living in a spiritual war—where unseen forces influence systems, shape perception, and govern the course of this present age. Yet the battle is not fought through human strength or natural effort. It is not fought in the flesh. It is fought in the spirit.

For this reason, believers are not called to react; they are called to remain watchful and anchored in prayer.

"Watch and pray, that ye enter not into temptation: the spirit indeed is willing, but the flesh is weak."
— Matthew 26:41 KJV

Because the adversary does not operate openly, but strategically seeking access through distraction, deception, and unguarded places of the mind.

"Be sober, be vigilant; because your adversary the devil, as a roaring lion, walketh about, seeking whom he may devour."
— 1 Peter 5:8 KJV

This is why discernment is necessary.

Not everything that appears natural is without influence.
Not everything that feels harmless is without effect. And not every battle is visible.

"My people are destroyed for lack of knowledge, because thou hast rejected knowledge, I will also reject thee, that thou shalt be no priest to me..."
— Hosea 4:6 KJV

www.ingramcontent.com/pod-product-compliance
Lightning Source LLC
LaVergne TN
LVHW010649110826
845149LV00014B/3007